COLLEGE:

HOW TO
GET THERE
&
GO FREE!

Fifth Edition

By

Idalah D. Womack

M.S.W., P.T.S., L.C.S.W.

Enlightenment Publications
Philadelphia, Pennsylvania

Since 1978

Copyright © 1999 by Idalah D. Womack

ISBN 0-7414-0524-5

Published by:

Infinity Publishing.com
519 West Lancaster Avenue
Haverford, PA 19041-1413
Info@buybooksontheweb.com
www.buybooksontheweb.com
Toll-free (877) BUY BOOK
Local Phone (610) 520-2500
Fax (610) 519-0261

Printed in the United States of America

Printed on Recycled Paper

Published January-2001

TABLE OF CONTENTS

i

TABLE OF CONTENTS

TABLE OF CONTENTS

PLAN
For the Future

"Believe in yourself, your neighbors, your work, your ultimate attainment of more complete happiness. It is only the farmer who faithfully plants seeds in the spring, who reaps a harvest in the Autumn."

B. C. Forbes

CHAPTER ONE
"HIDDEN FINANCIAL AID WORKSHOPS"

Since 1978, thousands of grants seekers such as you have attended "Hidden Financial Aid Resources" workshops presented at many colleges, universities, churches and high schools.

This data is based upon those workshops and the tremendous response from high school students, perspective students in addition to current undergraduate, graduate, professional and post-graduates.

Parents, grandparents and other relatives come to get information for their loved ones. In addition to higher education grants sources, participants said they got many ideas about areas of future employment.

If your college studies are to prepare you for work, you need to know where there are employment shortages. You may want to change your course major or add minor subjects helpful toward your gettting a job after college.

Responses to the workshops were actually overwhelming. Often, there was only standing room. Why did people attend? Most students said they needed money to start or finish college.

Some were seeking data that could have directed their educational course work in terms of what grantors were funding.

Others had thoughts of doing course work in subject areas that have become extinct such as many languages or special education programs that have been significantly downsized at some colleges.

Many said their high school teachers and counselors told them there were no funding opportunities for them. At that time, there certainly was grant money available. It was the same then such as now. Opportunities are inceased

1

COLLEGE: HOW TO GET THERE AND GO FREE
when the criteria match your demographics.

College Education: How To Get There And Go Free. Fifth Ed., (2000). **Chapter One** encompases data highlighted in "Hidden Financial Aid Workshops." It provides an overview of this book's contents. It is intended to give you information usable for the rest of your lives.

You will be able to seek, find, match, apply for and increase your chances of getting free help in educational pursuits. You, loved ones and friends must take advantage of this information now...and use it forever until free grants become extinct.

Chapter Two is a comprehensive review of the **History of Higher Education** in the United States of America. It is included so you will not be ashamed as many students say they are about applying for free money.

If you see all of the laws related to the origin of college subsidies, you also should want to benefit from them. Many colleges and public universities have educated some of its students by subsidizing all or part of their higher education costs.

Either your own or your parents' taxes have possibly paid for others to attend college. You also may be a recipient of good fortune relative to education subsidies.

When research was started for the first edition of this book, in 1973, it was approached with the excitement and wonderment of a discoverer or an explorer.

Some students said during their searches, school counselors had ruled out college for them and they wanted to try anyway.

How does one enroll in college? The segment about locating, surveying criteria and applying for free college grants was always evaluated among the most important data for workshop participants.

What was uncovered then and recently is being shared with you. More grant sources are provided to people than we are aware. Over one million college students receive free grants for tuition, room and or board, books or fees each year. Why not you? Why not you??? During the research for this book, many discoveries were made and they will be shared with you chapter after chapter.

While attending the workshops, some participants realized for the first time, there are numerous free grants available to us. You hear about them on television, radio. Others are seen on the internet and in newspapers.

People remembered hearing of friends, relatives or others who have received free scholarships, grants and subsidies. The problem was--no one told them or me how to find financial help. Many people were enlightened.

The value of this information is demonstrated by Temple University's housing previous editions in their archives located in Philadelphia.

Have you wondered for a long time about **Steps to College**? If so, read **Chapter Three** and get strategies and tips about what is necessary to apply and get accepted.

Chapter Four is **Where To Find Information About Free College Money**. It is a listing of various places you can find free, non-repayable grants offered by businesses, corporations, foundations, private sources and others.

One gentleman, who headed a program for Veterans at the University of Pennsylvania, wanted to prove the reliability of all of the locations where grants can be found. So, he went to each of those suggested in a previous book edition. He found the sources.

Yes, now he is a devout believer. More important, he has either gotten or enhanced his research skills. Today, using the same leads will contribute to your success in electronic searches on the internet.

Your following the ideas for finding grants sources as they are shown in this book will give you life-long skills. They especially will be helpful during hard economic periods in life.

Chapter Five: How To Increase Your Grant-Getting Opportunities has sections to help you organize your steps toward your grants search.

Students frequently say they are afraid of the questions asked on applications and whether I can show some of them in this book. This section suggests when and how to request an application from grantors. It is intended to alleviate fear. Listing the most asked questions on grantors' applications.

The recommendations are designed to help you increase your chances of getting free money for higher education in either grants, scholarships or fellowships. A sample Letter to use for Requesting an Application from Grantors has been included. It is in response to students who ask, "What should I write in the letter?"

Chapter Six shows the **Educational Progression** levels from high school through post-doctorate. You can see and plan the steps necessary to get to the top!

Grants Section is in Chapter Seven. It encompasses more than 400 grants that will get you started with your grants search.

Lists with the grantors' name, address and telephone numbers including fax and e-mail data are provided to you when they are provided by the source. Also, names of contact persons with application deadlines are shown. Criteria for applicants are listed for you. Grants are in alphabetical categories.

They are listed first by the grant number and then according to their page numbers. Added to the list are general grants without restrictions. Others are with restrictions such as: general grants for high school students, undergraduates, graduates, post-graduates, professionals, doctoral, post-doctoral.

Grants are available to specificethnic and culturally

4

diversegroups. Course listings are literally from A - Z. Some grants are specific to people with disabilites, medical students, etc. Thereafter is an extensive compilation of grants sources specific to Women, Graduates and Post-Graduates. Seeking travel? Travel/Study Abroad should interest you.

Chapter Eight is the **College Survival Guide**. It is written especially for the student who is the first in his or her family to attend college. If you are like me, I appreciated any help or suggestions the upper-class students such as graduates, seniors or juniors would share. Good suggestions assist you in saving very valuable time and your money.

You can thereby spend additional hours improving your work before it is due. I had no family help and 85% of my work was trial and error.

With guidance, efforts to attain high grades and the overall college experience would have been less grueling. Semester after semester, my spare time and money were spent buying and reading college "how to" books. Unfortunately, not one gave me legitimate strategies I could use over my 9 years of student life.

Many previous clients have either called or written to share their feelings about the helpfulness of the following College Survival Information.

It is included in this guide to increase opportunities for your becoming a college graduate. I love you. I want to guide you to success by giving you accurate, reliable and proven information.

Hundreds who have read and used the suggested Guide for College Survival have reported to me and staff that all of the tips actually worked for them too.

My niece Patrice, who read and used the book, said the ideas provided her additional academic standing at a suburban Ivy League College.

Often, refer to and use this Section, and you will say,

that information really assisted me. Rather than , "Where was this valuable, enlightening information when I was in college?

Read this book, then learn the various tasks. They will increase your chances for obtaining A and B grades in your course work. You need to know of "Hidden Financial Aid"and many other resources. Strategies discussed are to help you compete and win that college diploma.

In the **Appendices,** you will find the following: **Indexes Of Grants Subjects/Categories; Grants Sources; and a Bibliography Of Financial Aid Directories.** The extra data are resourceful because they tell you where you literally can find millions ($1,000,000s) of dollars of sources for college money .

Acknowledgments

I have eternal gratitude for blessings bestowed by the Creator of all things.

Deep appreciation goes to Dr. Mary Arnold-Frazier who was the first person to ask me, "What are you going to do after graduation from high school?" Then, at age 16, I wouldhad never thought of an academic future.

If Dr. Frazier (barely past her teens and already a teacher) had not challenged me to think, I guess, I would have settled for a job categorized as women's work during those years.

After sharing her very high mental abilities, Dr. Frazier forced me to push my mind and become dedicated to what has become a lifelong learning experience.

Now, I challenge pre-teens to begin thinking about various careers and the steps necessary to attain them. Help young people by your asking them about future aspirations. What are their choices and what steps are necessary to get where they want to be 10 years in the future?

Thanks also to Hamisi Tarrant, Erika, Nelson IV, Ciarra and Austin Durham, Lashauna Myers plus other young people such as Regina Sclafford who support people by volunteering to assist in any way those who are providing community services.

Gregory E. King must be commended for his patience and tolerance. He remained pleasant throughout my many questions about using computer technology for this desktop production.

Indeed, I wholeheartedly appreciate Antoinette Cummings and Eva M. Givens for their excellent proofreading and editing skills.

Also, thanks to Lula Davis and NoraHodges for their strong spirits of perseverance approaching 90 years of age--and to Anna Gland who is almost 100.

"Whoever you are or whatever you are doing, some
kind of excellence is within your reach."
- John W. Gardner

"If things are going against you just now, remember:
This, too, shall pass away." ---Kenneth Hildebrand

CHAPTER TWO

HISTORY OF FEDERAL LEGISLATION EFFECTING PUBLIC HIGHER EDUCATION

Grants Programs Starting With The National Association of State Universities and Land-Grant Colleges.
Founded in 1887, the National Association of State Universities and Land-Grant Colleges (NASULGC) is America's oldest higher education association.

It is a state voluntary association of public universities, land-grant institutions and many of the nation's public university systems.

Currently, there are more than 174 universities affiliated with NASULGC. For a list of all services available for United States of America's citizens, write to the NASULGC at One Dupont Circle, Washington, DC 20202.

Progression of Higher Education legislation is as follows:

1787 Northwest Ordinance is passed, authorizing the sale of public land for support of education, thus establishing the land-grant principle.

1862 The First Morrill Act is passed and signed by President Abraham Lincoln.

1887 The Hatch Act is passed, mandating the creation of agricultural experiment stations for scientific research.

1890 The Second Morrill Act is passed, providing further endowments for colleges. Part of this funding is to be used for institutions for black students, leading to the creation of 17 historically black land-grant colleges.

1907 Nelson Amendment to the Morrill Acts of 1862 and 1890 is passed, providing further increased appropriations to land-grant institutions.

1914 The Smith-Lever Act is passed, providing federal support for land-grant institutions to offer educa

9

tional programs to enhance the application of useful and practical information beyond their campuses through co-operative extension efforts with states and local communities.

1934 Congress creates the National Youth Administration to enable college students to earn money by performing educationally useful tasks and to continue their studies.

1935 Bankhead-Jones Act adds to annual appropriations for land-grant institutions.

1942 The General Equivalency Diploma (G.E.D.) program and the Military Evaluations Programs for veterans who left school to serve in World War II are established.

1944 Servicemen's Readjustment Act (G.I. Bill of Rights) Public Law 346 provides for the higher education of veterans.

1945 The Bankhead-Flannagan Act furthers the development of cooperative extension work in agriculture and home economics.

1946 Congress passes the Fulbright Act (Public Law 584) to enable Americans to study and teach abroad.

1946 The United Nations Educational, Scientific and Cultural Organization (UNESCO) is established, which among its many other activities, provides international exchange opportunities for American scholars and administrators.

1948 The U. S. Information and Educational Exchange Act (the Smith Mundt Act) provides for the international exchange of teachers, students, lecturers and other specialists.

1950 Point Four Program is enacted by Congress (the Foreign Economic Assistance Act, subsequently called the international Cooperation Administration, then renamed the Agency for International Development, or AID).

1950 Congress creates the National Science Foundation (NSF).

1950 The Land-Grant Endowment Funds Bill protects

federal and private endowments from unilateral federal action to divert them from the purposes for which they were granted.

1952 Veterans' Readjustment Assistance Act (Korean G. I. Bill of Rights) was passed.

1958 Higher Education Assistance Act becomes law with support from President Eisenhower.

1959 National Defense Education Act (NDEA) provides college student loans, graduate fellowships and aid for the improvement in the teaching of science, mathematics and modern languages that do not discriminate on the grounds of race, color, religion, or national origin."

1961 Report of the U. S. Commission on Civil Rights, "Equal Protection of the Laws in Public Higher Education: 1960" recommends that federal funds be disbursed "only to such publicly controlled institutions of higher education that do not discriminate on grounds of race, color, religion, or national origin."

1963 The Higher Education Act (HEA) of 1963 recognizes federal responsibility for aid to colleges and universities in the form of grants and loans for the construction of academic facilities.

1964 The National Defense Education Act Amendments authorize major changes to expand and strengthen the graduate fellowship program and eliminate discriminatory institutional limitation on loan-fund grants.

1965 The Higher Education Act of 1965 is passed funding many higher education. programs including student aid.

1965 Housing and Urban Development Act of 1965 establishes a maximum interest rate of three percent for the College Housing Loan Program to provide relief for students from the high cost of college attendance.

1966 The National Defense Education Project is passed to coordinate the federal role in international education

Education Act.

1979 The United States Department of Education was founded.

1980 Congress passes the Education Amendments of 1980 (to the Higher Education Act of 1965).

1991 National Security Education Act (Boren Bill) is enacted to provide support for undergraduate study abroad and graduate work in foreign languages and area studies.

1992 President Bush signs the Higher Education Act Amendments, reauthorizing the 1965 Higher Education Act.

1993 The National and Community Service Trust Act establishes a corporation to coordinate programs resulting in students receive minimum wage stipends and tuition benefits in return for community service.

1993 The federal government enacts "direct lending" as a program that enables colleges and universities to provide loans using federal funds directly to students, thus avoiding private lenders and streamlining the process.

Dawn of The Twenty-First Century.

Three decades since the adoption of the Higher Education Assistance Act of 1958, has brought drastic changes in the laws governing higher education subsidies.

Federal government grants have been shifted from an era of paying tuition, room and board, books and student fees to paying less than one half of all costs paid in behalf of students.

Thanks to President Dwight Eisenhower who thought that there was a need to give all Americans an opportunity to pursue higher education.

Increased education, he thought, would provide our nation an opportunity to compete with Russia and its Sputnik space exploration. The result was the first national program to assist students in getting financial aid grants.

Since the inception of the Higher Education Assistance Act, we have been able to successfully launch our own ma chines and robots into the new frontier. Thereby, the more America's space projects expanded, there has been a diminishing need to educate the masses.

The criteria for providing free grants and scholarships to students shifted from giving financial aid to those who had an interest in college, to people who had a need and then to demonstrated-need situations.

Now, federal subsidies are targeted to students from financially deprived families. Most subsidized programs have evolved to become repayable loans.

The 1960s and 1970s provided students 13 free government grants that paid from part to all of their tuition, room and or board, books costs, student fees, etc.

In the 1980s programs were reduced to 7. Other changes were influenced by William Bennett, Secretary of Education.

He stated on national television how the federal financial aid programs had little money left because people with adjusted gross incomes of more than $75,000 annually had taken advantage of the money that was geared toward those with far less resources.

Currently, the number of college tuition support programs is down to 5. President Clinton and congress have passed an increased higher education budget for 1997-98.

The additional funds are for Pell Grants to low-income students or Work/Study programs. What's the bottom line? Most grants programs were not created to pay all of your college costs.

The result is, you will possibly have a need to work during your college years unless you find free grants and scholarships that will.

They will be alternatives to federal and other government sources. Thus... the reason why *College Education: How To Get There And Go Free . 5th Ed., (1999).* is of great importance to you.

"I will study and get ready, then, perhaps my chance will come. Abraham Lincoln

CHAPTER THREE

STEPS TO COLLEGE

A statement for parents.

Sources listed in Chapter 6 were placed in this book to get you started on your grants searches and requesting applications. The sources help you learn how to conduct your search at the library and other locations.

This book, with more than 400 grants sources, is a very small fraction of monetary offerings you will find when you follow the strategies in **Chapter Five to Increase Your Grant-Getting Opportunities.**

Will you please commit your time and energy to assisting your teen or an older sibling by helping him or her find free money for college? Sometimes the grantors guidelines go out of date. Others may not respond to requests for applications. Thereafter, youths get discouraged and they may stop their grants search.

I want to strongly state to you that this is the only book about free higher education grants and scholarships that tells you exactly how to go to the library and other places to find hundreds of thousands of grants sources.

This topic has been researched by me for over twenty-five years. Trust me, these ideas and strategies can be used for gathering other resources. The skills you will learn are likely to be useful for the rest of your life.

My student years were spent searching and groping for free grants sources after my own scholarship source had closed. I looked for help like this. All books gave me lists but none told me how I could virtually find free money. This information is especially valuable if you find that the grant source you rely upon has moved with no forwarding address.

Also, none of the other sources gave me valuable life-long skills such as those that are developed from following steps discussed in this book. Take heed. This data is very important and it should be taken seriously.

Sources added to this book may change addresses or grants categories and some may actually be terminated; but, the process continues.

Other books will have you buy their updated grants books every two or three years. This one tells you how to conduct grants searches with details. Once you learn the process, you will never have to buy another book like this. In this regard, I am indeed an advocate for students.

This is my personal commitment because I had such a hard time with funding and academic advice when I was a student .

Benefit from my many mistakes!

Parents, please follow through on the suggestions made in this book. Increase your loved ones' chances of getting free higher education money and your opportunities to save thousands.

Message for high school students.

During tenth grade, go to your high school's guidance department and ask to see their higher education references such as the directories of colleges and financial aid sources. Let your guidance counselor know you plan to go to college and you need his or her assistance.

School staff.

Visit the Guidance Department . Counselors and school libraries have college information. The counselor will tell you to begin studying samples of previous questions asked of students on Scholastic Assessment Test Scores (SAT). Set aside four hours weekly to review mathematics and English tasks. Maximum scores in each are 800 and a perfect total is 1,600. Higher scores suggest that you will probably be able to successfully complete your college work.

Some youths have told me that they doubted whether any one can get a perfect 1,600 on the S.A.T.s but there are many lower scores such as 1,000 alone will not keep you from attending some colleges.

Especially, if you have a strong background of other activities such as sports, community activity, volunteer services, clubs, etc. They increase your opportunities for getting into college when you have high grades and the abilities to well-manage your time to successfully do many things.

Also, when you read the college directories, check whether the college or university of your choice is listed as not competitive, competitive or very competitive. Less academic work will be required at each of the levels.

When providing Hidden Financial Aid Resource Services Workshops, students of higher learning always requested steps and strategies to starting institutions higher learning. Will you need money to pay for your higher education?

Once your college selection process is started, apply for grants and scholarship consideration in 10th - 12th grades. Your guidance department and public libraries have many references for you to review for free grants.

They will either pay part or all of your expenses. You will have your college tuition paid for you immediately upon beginning your freshman semester.

All new college students.

Changing technologies will force workers of the future to know computer operations. Demands on the workforce include rapid innovations. Becoming employed other than in the service sector will require many of us to continue taking courses and learning new skills until we are retired.

Many continuing education programs have used the

name Lifelong Learning Programs and it accurately describes exactly what workers will be needing until we are retired.

Finding a college.

One key question from thousands who have been participants in the Hidden Financial Aid Resources Workshops ask is "How do I get started with higher education?"

Go to a library.

Get some of the college reference directories that list varied data about colleges. Find out about trade schools, technical studies, demographic data about students, the cost of tuition room and board, student fees, degrees available, campus activities, regulations, etc. The information can be found in your high school, college or public libraries.

Ask for the reference section.

Request permission to use the library's Internet and get online with universities' homepage and website addresses. They are regularly sent to libraries.

Otherwise, over the phone, mention to the librarian the department of the field you want to study. Write the name of the person to whom you are speaking in your data book.

If you ever need to talk to anyone in the information section again, ask for that person first when you make future calls.

Decide where you want to attend.

What college or university you want to attend? You can conduct your college search on the Internet by calling the federal government and getting the Website code for the Library of Congress or libraries with national college directories such as the College Board in New York City.

Now that you have gathered your list of 3-5 college names addresses, telephone numbers and names of contact persons, call, write, or visit the college to request an application for admissions.

When you know your major.

Call the department related to your field of interest. Ask for an adviser in that department. If you do not get an adviser, ask the secretary about the application process.

Request an application for admission to the department.

If you are going to major in music...get your materials from the music department, if its math, call, write or visit the math department. Campus of your choice is nearby? Visit and get your face known.

Remember to always give your name and address. Often, clients write or call me for information and then forget to include their addresses either on the envelope or within their letters.

Others call and forget to leave their phone numbers. Make it as easy as possible for people to send information that is helpful to you.

Sometimes there is uncertainty about a major. In this situation, you call the college's main admissions phone number. Ask the receptionist for a general admissions application.

Begin meeting people.

It is advantageous for you to visit the department(s) of your major or courses you want to take as soon as possible. You never know who may be of assistance to you.

Making allies may help you get the last placement slot for acceptance because of reviewers and other staff recognizing your name and face. This is especially helpful when you need to get into an over-enrolled course. The professor may be willing to add just one more student.

Whatever your needs, it is best to introduce yourself to as many college or university related people as soon as possible...you increase your chances of getting what you want at a time that it may be least expected.

You will continue to add names to your list of resourceful people who give you college-related information and help.

Admission Application.

When the application package arrives, read everything you receive once. Then, at a later time maybe after several days, read the instructions and take notes. Pay particular attention to the due dates.

Pace yourself and try to mail your data with the requested number of copies within several weeks ahead of the deadline. If for any reason, your packet is incomplete, you will have allowed yourself ample time to add whatever is needed.

Most application packages include: admission application forms: financial aid forms, three or more blank letters of recommendation forms and envelopes, a catalog of college programs and courses, and a form for writing your entry-essay explaining why you want to go to college.

All application forms should be entirely completed, honestly, and with brief statements. i. e. Questions vary from one institution of higher education to the next.

Some of the questions you will be asked are the following: Why did you choose your field of study? What past activities do you have that you feel are related to your educational emphasis or valuable to you?

Responding to application questions is uncomplicated when you focus on one question at a time. You will overwhelm yourself if you try to think about the whole application at the same time. Answer each question as thoroughly as possible.

Plan your answers so that there will be nothing that the application reviewers will have to contact you for to get additional data or clarification of your responses. Be direct and make your statements as short as possible.

Stay away from fluff adjectives and words. When

writing, speak plain and use words that are simple and jar-gon free. Some of our words are local slang or if they are technical, they may have many meanings, think in terms of less being more.

If you have difficulty with application questions, ask for assistance at the college admissions office. Are there any tips or key statements to add and increase opportunities for being selected? May you call again if you need information or help understanding a question?

Double-check and correct grammatical errors. There should never be more than one typographical on each page.

Application Fees.

When you pay fees with your application, the higher education institution keeps the fees whether you are accepted or not.

Some colleges annually receive hundreds of thousands. If fees are a hardship, some colleges will permit you to have them waived. Make the request at the admissions office prior to your sending the application.

If each one paid $25.00 for filing fees, then that institution received $2,500,000. Two and one half million dollars is money that can go into the discretionary college scholarship fund.

Work experience.

Do you have a resume? It will be a good idea to include one in your application package. The college admissions boards will have more information about you.

Also, this is where you highlight all of your academic as well as non-academic activities, volunteer work, church, temple or synogogue experiences such as services to the poor, elderly or people with disabilities.

Awards and Honors.

List any school, clubs community activities, volunteer work, etc. that awarded you various certificates, trophies,

pins, etc.
Verify your grades.

You will be asked to contact your high school and ask to have a copy of your transcript sent to where you are applying. An official transcript is sent from the high school directly to the school because sometimes students have tampered with and falsified their grades.

Now, institutions of higher learning may take a copy of a transcript from a student; but, no paperwork will be completed without the verification coming directly from the high school or a previous college or university.   The cost may be several dollars.
Financial aid applications.

In the application package, there is usually data relating to financial aid. President Bill Clinton's "Paper Reduction Act" requires very few forms that are used for university discretionary grants as well as local, state and federal financial aid programs.

Forms all students must file are: Free Application For Student Aid (FAFSA) and or Graduate And Professional School Financial Aid Service (GAPSFAS).

Stick to your tasks and obligate yourself to returning the completed papers as soon as possible.

In addition to due date requirements, there are other requests of grantors.   There is an income-contingent plan. If your income exceeds a specified sum, you may receive either the minimum or no grant.

Your family size will be considered with your debts. Remember to add your commuting costs, average weekly spending money, clothes purchases and bills. Also include the costs of your dry cleaning, shoe repairs, food, etc.

If no financial aid application is included with the institution's application forms, you call or visit the financial aid office at the higher education institution where you are applying.

Ask for financial aid forms to find whether you are eligible to receive financial aid subsidies offered by federal, state, local or other sources.

Be patient and get into a habit of monthly looking for scholarship money throughout high school from tenth-grade and then throughout college and graduate school. Go as far as you can on higher education grants... I did.

Post-graduate work was recently completed and paid for by a Department of Education Scholarship to specialize in work with people with disabilities. There could have been no greater opportunity for me. Since the 1970s, I have worked with children in special education classes.

While you are conducting your grant search, you also can weekly spend an hour or two seeking information about the college you want to attend.

Letters of Recommendation.

Within your application packet, usually 3-5 forms will be provided for you to give to people who will be asked to respond with no reservations that they are recommending that the college or university will accept you.

The data requested includes questions such as the following: how long the people have known you; the capacity of their knowing you; a statement about your academic ability and communications skills. The respondent will be asked to list qualities they have observed or recognized about you.

Seek only those with whom you have a good rapport or relationship. The persons may be a former teacher, guidance counselor, church affiliate, club leader, or someone in your community.

Do not ask anyone with whom you have an argument or some other disagreement to write these very important letters for you.

People who write the letters will have in their instructions that they are to seal them. Then they will either return them to you or send them to the college or university where they will be filed.

As a courtesy and so there will be no thought of your tampering with the data, put stamps on the envelopes and request that your respondents mail the letters.

It is unfortunate; but, so many students have looked at their letters and or have tried to change them. The result is the rules have become very strict about the recommendation envelopes being sealed after they are written.

When your completed application arrives, the letters of recommendation will be placed in your folder with your application materials in the admissions office.

Transcripts.

You will be asked to call your high school and or previous college to have a copy of your transcript(s) sent to the higher education institution where you are applying.

Photocopy, photocopy, photocopy!!! Maintaining Documents.

Before sending in your materials, please photocopy everything . When you graduate, you will recognize very soon your keeping copies of all transactions, papers, examination blue books, etc. is among the most important favor in college and all of life you can do for yourself.

Keep your papers together by years. Yearly, use one large envelope to add data until the next year. When there is a question about something that was done in the year 2002, you will be able to go directly to the envelope for that year and pull out your marked and returned work, transcripts and receipts, etc. Any previous student will tell you, it is likely you will need papers many times more than once.

Return your applications.

Send your applications in the fall of your senior year if you are in high school. Undergraduate students need to send their information by the due dates stated by their col leges. Often, it is required by March 1, of the year (September semester) they plan to attend college.

Attach your application fee to the front of your application. If you cannot afford to pay, ask your guidance counselor about getting an application fee waiver.

You can also request that the admissions application fee is waived, inquire at the admissions office about this. Some colleges report that applications submitted with an additional copy of all materials will be evaluated first.

You may want to make 3 additional copies of all application materials. Include a self-addressed,stamped, envelope (S.A.S.E.) or a postal card and the college or university will use it to notify you that your application has been received.

Recent higher education data reported that approximately 70% of all applicants are accepted to higher education. So...be calm, while you await your acceptance letter.

Some students apply to several colleges and universities simultaneously to maximize their chances of being selected to enroll at one or more and they pick and choose among them.

It is your option to increase acceptance possibilities. Now that you have been accepted, you must get organized and plan your next steps.. Many   helpful strategies are listed in the **College Survival** section in **Chapter Eight. Catalogs of courses and programs.**

Carefully read the catalog that lists all of the courses, rules and regulations that pertain to your major. Also pay attention to the general overall campus programs for all students. Many money-saving tips, scholarships, grants, internships, etc. are listed in many college catalogs.

Make sure you keep a copy of the catalog that was issued the semester you started college.   Sometimes curriculum is changed for various major studies and you will not have to take the added courses if they were not listed the catalog at the time you started higher education.

Your catalog can always be used to challenge whether you should take one or more additional courses to fulfill the requirements for your degree.

Pay attention to this information when you become a senior and if you are held back from graduating because one or more courses have been added to your major field of study, you will have back up data to support your claims.

When you can prove your requirements based upon cataloged data, you will go ahead and graduate and not have to spend additional time and money taking the courses.

Programs to exempt you from taking some courses.

You may have an opportunity to get credit for some of your required courses. If your work experience has taught you information that is similar to data required for a particular course fulfillment, you can take a test rather than sit in a classroom for 15 weeks or more.

Skills learned such as typing and data processing may meet the requirements for a business education course. Non-credit training in the military or other educational programs may qualify you for taking a College Level Examinations Opportunity C.L.E.O. test, fulfilling requirements for credits, paying for them and having less course work to do.

Knowledge gained during vacation or business trips may influence your passing a geography test. Pursue this little known opportunity.

Contact the closest public library and ask for forms to file for the C..L.E.O.) Program. When you pass the examination, you pay only the cost of the credits for that course and you do not have to take it and you will be graded for it. e.g. A course has four credits at $100 each or = $400.

If you pass the test for the course and pay the $400,

service is limited; nonetheless, it greatly saves time.
you get a passing grade and you go on to other course
work. Although the number of credits you can get in the
C.L.E.O.

International applicants.

People with outstanding English skills should apply
2-3 months in advance.

Adhere to due dates.

Some universities keep records according to the date
an application is sent and when it is returned. It gives review teams an idea about how long a student may procras-
tinate and wait to do follow-up with the course assignments.

Think about the student who would more impress
you...one who sends back the application in 5 weeks and
ahead of the due date or 5 months and after your stated
due date?

Essay response suggestions.

Essay questions vary from one institution of higher
education to the next. Most require either a personal or
autobiographical essay. Some of the questions you will be
asked are the following: Why did you choose your field
of study? What past activities and experiences do you have
that are of value and relate to your career choice?

Assess your strengths and weaknesses. List 5 or 6 of
your strengths, such as the following: You have good communication skills, research skills, finish what you start, are
dedicated to your beliefs, write well, you have leadership
abilities; although you have problems following other
leaders.

Essays are usually 500 words in length. Do not exceed
the recommended word restriction. Use your first two
paragraphs to state the four or five reasons that you want
to go to college.

Then, restate those reasons in one or two paragraphs

each in the order you wrote them in your thesis statement. I want to conduct research and advance my ideas, create new concepts and benefit many people in the areas of..." (add 2 or 3 paragraphs). Use words within your first two paragraphs to state the four or five opportunities college will provide you. Then, restate those reasons in one or two paragraphs each in the order you wrote them in your thesis statement. An opportunity to be creative will result in my... and that will assist my contributing... to the field of...(2-3 paragraphs).

Completing your entrance essay.

List one or two weaknesses e.g. You may not know when to stop making promises and you overdo responsibilities. Sometimes your opinions are too fixed and you do not allow new information to influence your modifying your thoughts about a particular topic.

Discuss how you plan to improve. An ability to face your shortcomings show your college reviewers you have insight and you do indeed make self-analyses.

Reviewers will recognize you are human, candid, flexible and you are growing. Be honest, no one is perfect. Staff on admissions review boards know you have failings too--they do, we all do.

Ending your essay-In conclusion, college will give me ...(repeat your beginning thesis statement). Increase my strengths by..., be of benefit to my community or society because of learning....decrease my weaknesses of ...etc.

In conclusion, this **Chapter Three** discussed how the following will assist anyone seeking information about how to get to college.

The necessary steps start with a statement for parents, benefitting from my mistakes, a message for high school students, school staff, all new college students, finding a college, go to a library, ask for the reference section, decide where you want to attend, when you know your major, begin meeting people, about the admission application, work experience, awards and honors, verifying your grades, financial aid applications, letters of recommendation, transcripts, resume, photocopy, photocopy, photocopy!!! maintaining documents, return your applications, catalogs of courses and programs, programs to exempt you from taking some courses, international applicants, adhere to due dates, essay response suggestions and completing your essay.

"If people empty their purses into their heads, no one can take it away from them. An investment in knowledge always pays the best interest"
Benjamin Franklin

"No race can prosper till it learns that there is as much
dignity in tilling a field as in writing a poem."
--Booker T. Washington

CHAPTER FOUR
WHERE TO FIND INFORMATION ABOUT FREE COLLEGE MONEY

Current and prospective students may visit the following locations to seek grants information. Ask for college grants directories, booklets, books, lists and manuals. Search for all grants sources in this chapter.

Academic fellowships.

Awards granted for graduate or postgraduate-level research and or education. It does not require repayment. There are sometimes visiting teacher opportunities where a professor at one college or university may transfer and teach for a specified amount of time at another. Contact college advisors for assistance.

Academic scholarships.

More than 1,200 of the 3,400 institutions of higher learning offer academic scholarships to students with B or better grade averages and Scholastic Aptitude Test (S.A.T.) scores of 900 or more. If your grades and scores are low, take an S.A.T. Preparation course to increase them. Pursue these with your guidance counselor.

Advanced placement programs.

Students who enrolled in college courses while they were still in high school benefited from this program. Others, with work experience related to the areas of college matriculation, may be eligible for the College Level Examination Opportunities (CLEO). Inquire at your advisor's office, student government or the public library.

Athletic scholarships.

Do you have above-average academic abilities? You may be good at golf, tennis, baseball, basketball, crew or lacrosse. Many colleges recruit students for varsity development. Call the financial aid office and ask for information about either a direct scholarship or a financial aid pack age.

Awards and honors.

These are given for academic achievement. They often consist of a total sum of money or a portion paid in annual increments to an institution of higher learning. They are for educational and related costs.

The grants do not require repayment. Go to the library and ask at the reference desk for all book lists of awards and honors for academic achievement.

Look in the catalogs of many colleges and see the various awards given. One or many may be based upon your qualifications. Request applications and apply.

Campus libraries-departmental.

Look in the library of the department where you have your major and be surprised to see data about free money to pay for college in the field you are studying.

Campus libraries--main.

Campus libraries have data about grants, scholarships and other free means of paying your higher education costs. Once again, go to the information or reference section and ask for their books, booklets and directories of college aid.

College catalogs.

Often, college and university libraries have data pertaining to other colleges and universities. Those catalogs most often list several grants that are available at those institutions.

In addition, there are others where you can nationally apply. This is an excellent source for grant-getting ideas. Ask at the library reference desk for catalogs of other higher education institutions.

Cooperative education.

Here is your opportunity to earn a grade and an income. You attend college for most of your course grades and you work for grades in businesses or services related to your major. Also, ask about learning and earning possibilities offered at the cooperative education office where you plan to complete your higher education.

Corporations.

One young man had a B average in high school biology classes. He wanted to major in biology but he had no money for college. He called Rohm &HaasPharmaceutical Company and asked about a college grant. He got one.

Four years of college education, book fees and commuting expenses were paid for by Rohm & Haas. The young man had to work for the company on Saturdays and for 2 years after graduation from college. In addition to free education, he was guaranteed a job for two years!

In a different situation, there was a junior in a business administration curriculum. She needed money to finish her senior year in college.

She called the International Business Machines (IBM) Corporation and discussed her needs. She explained how what she had learned in college to that point would benefit the company.

This particular student said she discussed her ideas that would benefit IBM and she was hired with subsidized tuition for her last year! Be assertive, ask for free grants that can be written off as corporate tax deduction.

Arrangements were made for her to get a grant with her promise to work for International Business Machines (IBM) Corporation for at least one year after graduation. During times of high unemployment, this was is an ideal scenario. Especially, when offers can lead to full-time employment.

Call the company hiring people who have expertise in the area of your choice of study or in fields related to your major. Find out about corporate grants to residents of your city and or community. Copies of their tax returns are available on microfiche. You can obtain them for a fee covering the copying expense. Call your local Internal Revenue Service office.

Department Of The Treasury, Internal Revenue Service.

If you have major corporations in your city, you may want to read copies of their income tax returns to determine whether the corporations have given free scholarships them for donations to colleges or Universities.

Directory of Million Dollar Companies.

Annually published by Dunn & Bradstreet, is a Million Dollar Directory. Copies can be found in the reference section of the public library. It is a compilation of all companies in America that made profits of over one million dollars during the previous year.

Call the corporations that hire employees with your educational major and request that you be considered for an educational grant...or...employment while you complete your higher education.

Directory Of Occupations And Titles.

This will help you determine your major as well as give you tips about what elective courses you should choose. If you are going to college to increase your employment opportunities, you need to read this book many times. Virtually hundreds of occupational titles have been eliminated since 1984. Read past and current issues to chart the changes of jobs over a 5-year period.

The directory will help you gear your education toward occupations that will be in high demand for people with your educational background. Otherwise, you will end up like thousands of students who annually graduate and find that they have no employment opportunities and they cannot get hired to do what they have studied.

Rather, many new graduates are taking jobs in fields totally unrelated to their four - six years of academic studies. Get this book at the reference desk of your free library.

Discretionary grants.

During my undergraduate education, I received a work study grant. My work included taking phone calls at the general receptionists' workstation. What was discovered was on several occasions weekly, many people called to set up trusts to make donations to the University.

Some grantors made discretionary grants that were arranged for the head of a department or another staff person to decide who should receive the (usually one-time) grant.

As long as the grantor can write off the grant as a donation to an educational institution, he or she may not be concerned who receives the generous gift. Ask your departmental advisor about the availability of these funds.

Enroute to the copier one day, I noticed on a bulletin board there was money available. Colleges and Universities have long had discretionary grants, scholarships and fellowships though very few people have known of them.

Encyclopedia Of Associations.

An excellent source of help to you is this listing of national associations. Included with a brief description are the names of contact persons, addresses and phone numbers.

If your major course of matriculation is art, dance, language, physical science, sociology or others, write their associations listed in the American and National Sections and request information about the availability of free grants and scholarships.

People who have completed college and received grants while they were students are more likely to share grant information with you. Their opportunities are not decreased or threatened because you are competing with them.

Ask for the community representative, public information officer or the public relations office (corporations have one).

Fellowships.

Awards granted for graduate or post-graduate-level research and or education that does not require repayment.

Government Printing Office.

Available to the public are many pamphlets and bibliographies providing information about free and other grants source books related to higher education. Also, an explanation about book content in addition to costs is provided.

Call your local federal building and or visit their government Printing Office. What is available to the public are catalogs and price lists with information about free and other grants source books related to higher education. An explanation about book content is provided

If you must write, request a copies of their catalog. A worker will send you a check-off booklet of available books and once its returned, your order will be filled. Education Department, Post Office Box 16, Pueblo, CO 81009.

Government-sponsored programs.

Federally subsidized programs have been implemented since the Higher Education Assistance Act of 1958 to help students. Write the Federal Student Aid Information Center, P. O. Box 84, Washington, DC 20044.

In some instances, grants are established and provided only at various colleges and universities. When you get the name of the grants sources, contact the college that is a conduit for that particular grant.

One of those institutions of higher learning may not have been among your original choices. You may want to relocate to have your academic costs, student fees, room, board, books, etc. fully paid for you.

You may change your mind about commuting or relocating to other states or cities when you have no out-of-pocket expenses.

Grades.

When you enter a course or higher educational program, the cost of your tuition is absorbed by the college or university. When your attendance is good and grades are "C" or better, you do not have to repay any debt and the cost is actually written off and subsidized for you.

If you get less than "C" grades, you may have to repay the cost of your loan to the grantor. Before accepting grants or loans, be sure to read and understand all of the rules, regulations, and requirements.

Greek-lettered organizations.

Look on campus for the sorority and fraternity organizations. Many can provide you information about Greek-lettered organizations such as fraternities or sororities.

Some people choose to pledge for Greek organizations that will give free grants and scholarships to their members.

Home equity. Homeowners accumulate unused equity in their homes. Your parents can release this equity either through a line of credit or by refinancing the first mortgage on a home. Contact the family bank or any other lending institutions.

Internet services.

If you have computer access and Internet either at school, where you work, in a library or at home, you can easily get grants information by typing in lowercase letters, words such as www.college grants.com. Otherwise, call colleges you know give grants and request their website or homepage addresses.

Some of those to assist you with your search are: www.fie.com, Scholarship Resource Network(SRN) www.rams.com, www. powerstudents.com, www. collegeedge.com,http://easi.ed.govwww.

COLLEGE: HOW TO GET THERE AND GO FREE

athletesguide.com, www.ihad.org, www.uncf.org, www.dogpile.com.

Loan forgiveness.

When your attendance is good and grades are "C" or better, you do not have to repay any debt and the cost is essentially written off for you. Less than "C" grades, you have to forfeit your loan. If you had to pay for your higher education costs via using loans, you may be willing to obligate yourself to working with designated populations to have portions of your loan annually "forgiven" or subsidized. Ask the representative of your loan source about this service.

Loans.

Money you borrow from a bank or other lending institution and you must repay with interest.

Medical opportunities.

Shortages of nursing and other medical personnel has caused money to be made available for full tuition, room and or board, book costs, travel, relocation-moving and other fees. Call hospitals, medical colleges and universities.

Military provisions.

Recent work with an Adult Basic Education revealed higher education supports provided for people who are committed to service in the National Guard.

There are some advantages such as federal bonuses, state benefits, student loans, partial loan forgiveness, drill pay and some tuition remission.

Look in the colored pages of your local phone book. That is where government department and services are listed. Other branches of the military also provide grants. Inquire at a recruitment station or office.

Public libraries-community branch offices.

Public libraries have books that are the same and similar to those in the immediate community. Branch offices offer somewhat different books.

If the middle-aged and youth populations live in a newly developed area of the city, then the majority of books at the branch office of the library will have a majority of books for the middle-aged parent(s) and youth groups.

Also, if a city's population consists of 60% senior citizens, 30% youth and 40% Mexican Americans, many of the books will reflect and be of interest to senior citizens, youths and Spanish-speaking people.

Public libraries-main branches.

These libraries have holdings based upon the general interests of the entire city or town. Ask for Business, Private, and Foundation Scholarship Books. In addition, request books for general grants for United States Citizens and specific categories such as counselor, education, engineering, golf, internships, law, mathematics, medical, etc..

Scholarship loans.

This is a scholarship that becomes a loan if the recipient does not comply with the terms of the scholarship.

Scholarships and grants.

Arrangements are made where financial aid requires no repayment and usually, the grantor pays part or all of the following: tuition for up to four years; undergraduate study; two years for graduate pursuits; doctorate and or dissertation fees, students' fees, books, supplies, living expenses (room and or board) and or other related costs.

Sociology departments.

Corporate and foundation giving tells us among other things, these entities have sympatico with the betterment of human kind. It is understandable that free grants and scholarships to people are either filed or cross-filed in the sociology section of libraries.

Look for data about college and vocational/technical sources in bookstores educational grants in the sociology section of the library or in bookstores.

Teachers' assistanceships.

Students who are seniors in undergraduate programs or in graduate school are often offered an opportunity to serve as teachers' assistants.

Teaching Assistantships usually are based upon academic merit and financial need. They are for students who will assist professors in exchange for financial assistance. Most often, this pays tuition. Sometimes assistanceships pay the costs of books and they allow for a small monthly stipend. The selected students may have to do no more than distribute test papers or blue books, collect test responses and or mark tests on occasion.

Request information about teachers' assistanceships months before starting your senior year or first year of graduate school.

Talk to your advisor, dean of your major (i.e. journalism, music, etc.) department or a teacher with whom you have established yourself as a student with A or B grades.

Tuition reimbursement.

Over the past decade, employees have made a conscious effort to choose jobs that offer free trade school or college education among other benefits.

During Hidden Financial Aid Workshops, Many people laugh when they are asked, "Have you thoroughly read your employment manual or packet?" Most people respond that they only read the portion that explains medical benefits and vacation days.

What is overlooked is the section describing reimbursements to employees for job-related course work. The employee has paid the costs for his or her courses before attending.

The company repays the employees for all or a percentage of course costs. Also, a minimum of a C - average must be maintained.

Other methods of payment are available. If you work in banking, at the end of the successfully attended and completed course, your tuition is either paid for you or returned to you.

You will have the opportunity to attend free, college-level course related to banking. You can learn bookkeeping, accounting, securities, etc. Banking courses are also offered free at the American Institute of Banking. It is arranged within a business school, college or university.

When you have job interviews with personnel representatives, ask questions about tuition reimbursement benefits or other supports for higher and continuing education.
Tuition remission.

Similar to the data stated above, people seek jobs where they receive free higher education tuition payments. The advantage is no restriction to only studying subjects directly relating to your job. You have options to study whatever you choose.

When you enter the course, the cost of your tuition is absorbed by the college or university. When your attendance is good and grades are "C or better, you do not have to repay any debt and the cost is essentially written off for you. This is especially the situation when you are a college or university employee.

Contact the personnel office, financial aid department, or Dean of the college or university where you are attending. Ask about the necessary process for tuition remission consideration.

If you already are a working student and find yourself running out of tuition money, ask for free college grants and scholarships' booklets, books, directories, lists and manuals. Your income after deductions may be over $12,000 or $35,000.

It may not stop you from getting a grant. In the opinion of a grantor who annually has more than $75,000,000.00

(75 MILLION DOLLARS) to give away, your income is a very small amount.

Never say you have or make too much money. Never discount yourself. Let the person from whom you are requesting help say you do not qualify.

You will always get more out of life and many surprises when your first thought is positive about everything.

Work-study grants.

Sometimes the National Defense Student Loan Program provides grant money to students who must work off the grant amount. i. e. If a grant is made for $1,000 the recipient must work for it. e.g. The student may find a campus job at $8.00 per hr. He or she may have to work 7 weeks ($960) and 5 hours ($40) to fulfill the requirement for up to $1,000. Contact your financial office for information.

In conclusion, you will find information about free college money by looking into the following: Academic fellowships, Academic scholarships, Advanced placement programs Athletic scholarships, Awards and Honors, Campus libraries-departmental, Campus libraries-main, College catalogs, Cooperative education, Corporations, Department of the Treasury-Internal Revenue Service, Directory of Million Dollar Companies, Directory of Occupations and Titles, Discretionary grants, Encyclopedia of Associations, Grades-Greek-lettered organizations, Home equity, Internet services, Loan forgiveness, Loans, Medical opportunities, Military provisions, Public libraries-community branch offices, Public libraries-main branch, Scholarship loans, Scholarships and grants, Sociology departments, Teachers' assistanceships, Tuition reimbursement, Tuition remission, and Work-study grants.

CHAPTER FIVE

HOW TO INCREASE YOUR GRANT-GETTING OPPORTUNITIES

Some grants are for general studies. You can major in a subject of your choice. Others are restricted grants and the grantee subsidizes specific fields or areas of studies, e.g. accounting, nursing, socialwork, etc.

While working in the university's copy center one day, a glance at a bulletin board in the psychology department revealed unexpected information. There was a note stating the department received a discretionary grant for $40,000. It was available for 10 students who wanted to study psychology. The very next day, the grant notice had been removed from the locked-glass bulletin board cabinet.

Later, I learned most public and public-private colleges have money budgeted and called discretionary funds. Inquire at the department where you want to major and throughout the university.

Use the checklist in this section to determine what grants to search according to your desires and demographics.

Grant criteria search questions based upon the most asked questions on grantors' applications.

After reviewing more than 1,000 applications for free higher education grants and scholarships, it was apparent most grantors give on the bases of one or more of the following: one individual can receive funding because of financial need; another may be awarded a scholarship because of scholarly grades; and others may be chosen based upon his or her gender, course major, religion, etc.

When you consider which variables apply to you, you will have found the right grantors based upon your qualifications to fulfill their criteria.

Examples:

The Epilepsy Foundation of America, offers scholarships to <u>Social Work majors</u> who are undergraduates and you must <u>do research</u> relating to <u>epilepsy</u>. You must apply by <u>March 1,</u> of each year.

or

The Kosciuszko Foundation offers educational grants to <u>Polish Americans</u>. Students must be <u>undergraduates</u> (college-level juniors and seniors) or <u>graduates.</u> They must either be <u>United States of America citizens;</u> of <u>Polish descent; Poles</u> with U. S. <u>permanent resident status; or Americans</u> pursuing the study of <u>Polish subjects.</u>

or

National Society of Public Accountants Scholarship Foundation awards scholarships to students <u>majoring</u> in <u>accounting</u> with "<u>B"or better</u> grade-point average. <u>Only undergraduate</u> students are eligible. You must be entering your <u>2nd year</u> of studies. Read the criteria thoroughly so you will not waste time and money corresponding with the wrong grant source. Remember, according to the United States Census Bureau, White Anglo-Saxon Protestants are listed under population demographics.

All other ethnicgroups are among those most people would not have considered minorities. If your ancestors migrated to America, or were force to come here, you may be eligible for various grants.

Review of the most asked questions by grantors.

The steps leading toward funding acceptance are below. Use the following questions and fine tune your grants search process and possibilities.Photocopy the sheets on the next pages and use them as guides during your next research outing. They will help you determine the many areas where you may qualify for grants.

Acceptance.

Most grantors want to know whether the applicant has

44

been accepted at an institution of higher learning such as a trade school, college or university.

Contact the admissions office where you plan to attend college and request a letter to be sent to the grantor. This verifies your enrollment. If you are in high school, applying early beforegraduation, tell the grantor. Your application may bepending approval. A check usually will be held for you until the admissions process is completed.

Age.

Until this decade, the majority of grants researched were generally available to people 18-35 years of age. Now, many are provided to college-bound high school students thru peoplewho are senior citizens.

Community involvement.

Often, leadership grants and scholarships are offered to people who may have helped get a traffic light in the neighborhood or helped change some social policy.

Politicians especially sometimes give up some of those grants and scholarships that they receive upon election and few of us know about them.

Cooperative education.

Provides students opportunities to learn while they earn. Call the Cooperative Education Office on your campus or get information by sending a postcard to the National Commission for Cooperative Education, 360 Huntingdon Dr., Boston, MA 02115.

Request a copy of their current publication about the process for pursuing a cooperative education program. You save money. Also, you will get valuable working experience in addition to pay.

Course major.

Often, people who are successful in specific majors become wealthy. Some of those people either set up foundations or they give private grants to individuals pursuing the majors they had when they were college students.

If a grant is offered to people who study Sociology and you desire studying psychology, you may major in Sociology and minor in Psychology. You increase your grant-getting opportunities.

You still get many of your subjects in the field you want; yet, you also get free college money--you study what the grantor wants. What do you want to study?

Employment background.

Sometimes your employment experience increases your likelihood of getting free grants. This is especially true when course work is offered in a field with shortages of workers. New media is one. It is in high demand such as computer programmers used to be years ago.

Employment tuition programs.

When you enter a course, the cost of your tuition is absorbedeither by you or your job. When your attendance is good and grades are "C" or better, you do not have to repay any debt. The cost is written off for you.

If you get less than "C"grades, you may have to repay the cost of your grant. Before accepting grants, be certain you know all of the rules, regulations and requirements specified in the eligibility data.

Ethnic groups.

Although most people believe "minority groups" most often applies to Blacks, Latinos, Native American Indians and Asians, the terminology encompasses far more ethnic groups.

Go to the federal Department of Commerce in your city and ask to read census data. You will find under population that there is a numerical figure for white, Anglo-Saxon Protestants.

Then, the listing is for "other" ethnic groups and they do mean...all others. It includes: Aleut Americans, African Americans, Chinese Americans, German Americans, Hispanic Americans, Irish Americans, Italian Americans,

HOW TO INCREASE YOUR
GRANT-GETTING OPPORTUNITIES

Japanese Americans, Jewish Americans, Native Americans, Polish Americans, etc.

The Federal Government lists all groups other than white Anglo-Saxon Protestants as minorities. Thereby, unless you are a White Anglo-SaxonProtestant, you are a member of an ethnic group and you are eligible to apply for every grant provided to minorities unless pecific ethnic groups are noted.

Apply only if your ethnic group is stated. Write: The Department of Education, Pueblo, CO. 81009. Ask for information about educational grants and scholarships. Request, if they do not have them at that time, whether they will refer you to other sources that do.

Exchange students.

Seeking an opportunity to study abroad? Your travel, room, board, tuition and fees are paid for you. Contact the office of Students' Affairs on your college campus. Otherwise, write the Ambassador to the country where you want to pursue higher education.

Write the Council for International Exchange of Scholars, Eleven Dupont Circle, NW, Suite 300, Washington, DC 20036.

Financial status: (check all that apply)

_____Need Money_____No Need

Gender. Due to shortages of college-educated men or women in various course majors, some grants will specifically be for people of one sex or another. Apply for these grants too.

Geographic residence.

There are numerous corporations providing free grants to people who live in a city where the main offices of those companies operate.

Call: Request the Community Representatives, the PublicInformation Office or PublicRelations Staff of Corporations and companies in your city and state.

47

Ask whether they give educational grants and scholarships. If they do not, ask whether they know of sources that do.

Grades.

Grantors sometimes prefer to give their money to students who attain only honor grades such as As or Bs. If you are not an honor student, do not apply for these grants.

Grades-honors.

There are many other grants based upon criteria for which you can apply. Honor Students should seek in addition to other grants, those made available by the American Mensa Scholarship Committee. The Address is 1701 West Third Street, Brooklyn, NY 11223.

Military or veterans status and benefits.

Providing Hidden Financial Aid Resources Workshops at various sites for veterans has been very rewarding. There is a great feeling when something is given back to those who gave so much protecting our lives.

What bothered me most when telling veterans about their many scholarship opportunities was their seldom knowing about them. Will you tell veterans there is money available for their free higher education pursuits?

Need.

Some initially poor people who have had opportunities to attend college have become millionaires. They give to students who demonstrate their need of college money. Tax returns or social service agency data may suffice.

Religion.

Ask the head of your church, synagogue,temple or masque for a list of national religious organizations. Otherwise, look for your religious denomination in the indexes of financial aid directories, booklets and books.

Some of those grants require you to study theology and others do not. Search for grants funding the criteria most matching you and your personal demographics.

HOW TO INCREASE YOUR
GRANT-GETTING OPPORTUNITIES

Your religious affiliate may offer financial aid assistance to your congregation. There are national religious associations offering financial aid support programs. Inquire at your site.

Restricted grants.

Reasons vary why grantors request specified criteria be met before grants are given to grantees. While searching libraries for this book, grants were seen for people who are sheep herders and others because some people had the same last name as the grantor.

Grants may have been because you played baseball or golf. Other grants are given to women because they are returning to higher education after giving birth.

Thoroughly check the required criteria and increase your grant-getting opportunities. Be mindful of some grantors changing their criteria every several years. Always be willing to do library research to update your data.

Specific colleges and universities.

Various institutions of higher learning offer grants only available at their college or university site. Before committing and attending an institution, check whether university grants are available.

If you receive a full scholarship or other grant paying your tuition, room board and student fees,you may choose one college or university over another.

Unions.

Members pay dues and they are often used for philanthropic services such as providing scholarships. They may be for members' children or those in a community where the union has its main activities. Ask where you work.

Volunteer work.

Grantors who have humane objectives have them fulfilled when they give free grants and scholarships. Sometimes favorably look upon others who are volunteers.

Remember, working with little league baseball; being

a den parent or scouts; or, helping with your religious activities may help you qualify. List that information and forget about being humble this one time.

Willingness to travel.

If there is a shortage of employable people with your
major living in certain geographic regions, you may be offered full tuition, room and board to relocate.

Information about financial aid services can be obtained
at libraries. College directories usually also list contact
people.Get directories at reference desk

Work-study programs.

This is an opportunity to receive specified loan amounts
and work off the entire sum. It is distributed over a number of pay checks and based upon an hourly wage.

Inquire at the college financial aid office.

**When and how to request an application for grants
sources.**

Immediately after stating the criteria requirements,
most grants listings will tell you of the deadline or due
dates. Before the date is when to submit applications.

If you exceed the date, your application will not be considered.

A short letter such as the sample on the next page can
be used to request an application. Your own similar letter
will get the same results.

Thoroughly read the criteria so you will not waste time
and money corresponding with the wrong grant source.
Search for sources funding people with your background
and personal demographics.

The tips in this chapter are for maximizing and increasing your success in getting grants opportunities. They are
from thevery generous corporations, foundations, government subsidies, private businesses and individuals within
our own American Country.

HOW TO INCREASE YOUR
GRANT-GETTING OPPORTUNITIES
DEMOGRAPHICS MATCH SHEET

Financial Status: (check one) Need Money__No Need__
Grades: - As + Bs _____**yes or no** _____ Do
not look for scholarships designated for scholarly students
if you are a C-grade student).
Courses_____,_____,
_____,_____.
Age: _____Many grants are restricted to high school
pupils. Others are specifically for people over age 55.
Gender (sex): _____ Some grants are specifically for either
men or women.
Ethnic Group: _____ These are often found listed in the
minority category.
Course Major: _____, _____,_____
Religion: _____ Various denominations offer
scholarships for parishioners studying divinity, theology
or a major of your choice.
Geographic Residence: _____ Some grants are made
to you because you live in a particular state or county.
Are you willing to travel? _____ If there is a shortage of
people educated in your major living in a certain state, you
may be asked to be educated there. Also, after graduation
you may be asked to work there for a number of years.
Volunteer Work: ___Grants are sometimes given to people
who have been generous with their time and or resources.
Other: Reasons vary for grantors to request specified criteria be met before grants are given to grantees. Check these
thoroughly and increase your grant-getting opportunities.

"You know much more than you think you know."
--Dr. Benjamin Spock

COLLEGE: HOW TO GET THERE AND GO FREE

Assess the data on the Demographics Match Sheet. Begin forming a profile of yourself. It will help youpursue grants because of many aspects of your life rather than just a few.

Write a short letter. Use the sample on the next page. Use it to request an application. Your own similar letter will get the same results.

In conclusion, there are grants available giving funding on the bases of each category and a combination of the above.

All you have to do is thoroughly read the grant criteria. Select sources funding the criteria you match with your own personal demographics. Otherwise, pass thegrant source on to a relative or friend who can use it.

Remember, adhere to deadline dates. They will be shown with the grants if the grantors provided them. You should reap many rewards by following the guidelines shared in this book.

Frequently, people get back to me and say, "I got several grants using your process..." Listen to me. Use the information in this book.

"Treat people as if they were what they ought to be and you help them to become what they are capable of being."
-Johann Wolfgang Von Goeth

HOW TO INCREASE YOUR
GRANT-GETTING OPPORTUNITIES
SAMPLE LETTER TO USE WHEN REQUESTING
GRANTORS' APPLICATIONS
(Your own or a similar letter will get the same results)

DATE_____

(Name of grants sources contact person. If it is not listed,
continue)
A.B.C. Foundation
22 Zero Street
Anywhere, USA

To Whom It May Concern:

I have information about your offering grants and
scholarships for individuals interested in higher education. I am requesting an application and any additional
data you provide.

One of your criterion is that I major in ... I have had
good to excellent grades in that subject. Your considering
me to receive a college grant will be appreciated.

Very truly yours,

Sign your first and last name

Type your first and last name

"Have patience. All things are difficult before
they become easy."   --- Saadi

COLLEGE: HOW TO GET THERE AND GO FREE

The suggestions provided in this section are intended to give you the greatest opportunities to receive free college education.

Use this data: Grant criteria search questions based upon the most asked questions on grantors' applications: Age, Community involvement, Cooperative education, Course major, Employment background, Employment tuition programs, Ethnic groups, Exchange students, Financial status, Gender, Geographic residence, Grades, Grades-honors, Military or veterans status and benefits, Need, Religion, Restricted grants, Specific colleges and universities, Unions, Volunteer work, Work-study programs, Demographic Work Sheet, Are you willing to travel? When and how to request an application for grants sources, and a Sample Letter To Use When Requesting Grantors' Applications.

"Although I came from a poor and humble background, I did not come from a family of people who had a poverty view of the world. I came from people who viewed the world as attainable." --Faye Watleton

CHAPTER SIX

EDUCATIONAL PROGRESSION

The steps to college begin after completion of high school or a general education diploma (G.E.D). The following data provides you information about the educational attainment steps.

They are necessary to accelerate to the next higher academic levels. Ultimately, accomplishment of the curriculum at each level leads to degrees.

First, there is the associate degree, then - undergraduate degree, internships, professional development, graduate degree, post-graduate education, doctorate degree, post-doctorate education.

Internships.

These provide work experiences with pay to learn in a specified field. Internships are for a specified amount of time, e. g. 3 weeks, 2 months, etc. They usually are offered by professional associations and large businesses. A stipend is included.

These arrangements will provide you training, work experience and monetary compensation. Internships give you an opportunity to work and earn money to help pay for school.

Some internships are available for pre-high school graduates and others are for undergraduate students or for those who have already attained the degree.

High School Diploma.

Requirements are based upon the completion of education at the secondary level above middle school.

General Education Diploma.

Call your neighborhood high school. It often offers a G.E.D. program because so many youths drop out of school In the urban areas, the number is approximately 50%.

Later, students realize they are in poverty. They cannot make much above minimum wage without a diploma.

Their fate is they become among the underemployed employed. Their salaries are not sufficient to pay a month's rent or mortgage from one pay.

The result is either homelessness or crime then living in institutions. Stay in school. Learn a trade or go on to college. Otherwise, you may become homeless in the future.

Professional development.

This is for course work taken to learn new methods of doing your job such as supervisory certificates, real estate licenses, etc. This person may or may not have or need degrees.

People who may not go to college, may have careers in professions. This level of education does not lead to a degree.

Undergraduate Degree.

Past graduation from high school and attained at a college or university, junior or community college level for two years of study that includes an associate degree; also, it includes apprenticeship/vocational and technical institutes that lead to bachelors degrees. Student Aptitude Test scores (S.A.T.)) are most often required.

Some undergraduate educational programs are on quarter sessions rather than attending college for 15-week sets of course work, you attend 3 months at one time and then have one or more months off before the next semester begins.

You may want to pursue these arrangements to meet work requirements, if you keep a job while attending college. You can progress from undergraduate to doctorate.

We are programmed to go from undergraduate, to graduate and then to doctorate. Think about how much money and time are saved by passing a 1-2 year graduate exam and not have to attend the otherwise required courses.

Graduate Degree.

Study leading to a Master's Degree such as M.A., M.S., M.S.W., L.L.M, etc. Never let a lack of funds keep you from pursuing graduate education.

If you were successful in undergraduate work, you will do well as a graduate student too. Many resources are available for this.

Inquire at your college department or the financial aid office about researching libraries and their directories. A prerequisite for this level of study is either the Graduate Record Examination (GRE), Graduate Management Admissions Test (GMAT), Law School Admissions Test (LSAT).

Post-graduate Education.

These are obtained after graduation from graduate school. You may continue taking courses although you will not matriculate toward the attainment of a doctorate's degree.

Doctorate Degree.

Academic acceleration beyond the graduate (postgraduate phase) level while working officially enrolled in a doctoral program will result in the attainment of the doctorate degree.

This is continuing education beyond the attainment of a doctorate degree. All first-time/beginning college students start at the level of an undergraduate.

Post-doctorate education.

This is the top level of higher education attainment. You are continuing education beyond the doctorate degree. Remember, you can begin your plight toward higher education from internships, high school diploma, G.E.D., professional development, associate degree, internship, -undergraduate, internship, graduate, post-graduate education, doctorate and finally a post-doctorate education.

Educational Progression

Post-doctorate Education

Doctorate Degree (est. $35-plus, plus, plus per hr.)

Post-graduate Education

Graduate Degree (est. $25-40-plus, per hr.

Internship

Undergraduate Degree (est. $15-$22 per hr.)

Associate Degree (est. $8.00 -$12 per hr.)

Professional Development
General Education Diploma (G.E.D.) (est. $5-$7 per hr.)
Internship

High School Diploma (estimated $6-$8 per hr.)

Internship
Grade School Thru 12th Grade Education

CHAPTER SEVEN

GRANTS SECTION

These sources assist in your developing and or improving assessment abilities you already have. You will be looking at criteria and whether they match you or a person with your individual background.

The purpose of this listing is to get you started with your matching demographics. In addition, you get an opportunity to develop a very positive attitude toward believing there are over 100s of thousands of sources. There is a likelihood you too, with persistence, can get a grant.

Grants sources are listed according to their numerical order. For a cross reference, you may use the grants index in the back of this book. Grants are in alphabetical order within categories and the page is also provided.

Pay attention to criteria as you have learned in previous chapters. Also, be certain to adhere to due dates. They are the deadlines for applications.

If you think yours will be late; do not ask for an extension. You do not want to anger or test the patience of someone from whom you are asking to give you money. Apply elsewhere.

Get applications early so you will respond by the specified deadline. Deadline dates will be shown with the grants if the sources provided them.

You will reap many rewards by following the guidelines shared in this book. Frequently, people get in touch and they say, "I got several grants using your process..." **Listen!!!** Use the information in this book. Avoid making the same mistakes as I.

Seek, And You Will Find:
There are more than 400 awards classified by specific

COLLEGE: HOW TO GET THERE AND GO FREE

grants categories. If no restriction is made pertaining to the field of study, it will be listed as a *general grant*. Levels of learning attainment are listed in the order that they usually are obtained.

This section gives you practice in scrutinizing grants sources and their criteria to perfect your search. Use the grants in the listings to familiarize yourself with grants sources, how they are listed and how to match your demographics with the criteria.

Sometimes the sources move or change their giving patterns, keep hope. If the sources change addresses or giving patterns...you have information to find thousands of other sources

After all, the purpose of the book is to get you to college. Add resources to pay for it. Graduate from higher education at least once. Use *Chapter Four: Where to Find Information About Free College Money* over and over and forever search topics to start you on the grant search toward your graduation.

BEST WISHES WITH YOUR SUCCESSFUL GRANTS SEARCH!

This One is For You...

"Leaving behind nights of terror and fear, I rise. Into a daybreak that's wondrously clear, I rise."
Dr. Maya Angelou

(001) Academic Merit Awards-Graduate. Scholarship Foundation of America, 55 Highway 35, Suite 5, Redbank, New Jersey 07701. Contact: Ellen Manning or Linda Paras. Awards averaging $1,000 for academic merit.

(002) Accountants. National Society of Public Accountants, Member Services Department, 1010 North Fairfax Street, Alexandria, Virginia 22314-1574 (703) 549-6400 Fax: (703)549-2984, 1 (800) 966-6679.

The NSPA Scholarship Foundation Board of Trustees awards an average of 22 scholarships per year in the amount of approximately $41,000 each for accounting students entering their third or fourth year of studies and approximately $500 each for students entering their second year of studies.

Outstanding students in the competition, designated the Charles H. Earp Memorial Scholar receives an additional award of approximately $200. Write or call for guidelines. Fax; (703) 549-2984, 1 (800) 966-6679.

(003) Accounting-Undergraduate. National Society of Public Accountants Scholarship Foundation. 1010 North Fairfax Street, Alexandria, VA 22314-1574, (703) 549-6400, Fax: (703) 549-2984.

The NSPA Scholarship Foundation offers scholarships to students majoring in accounting with a "B" or better grade-point average. Only for undergraduate students.

Annually, there are 22 scholarships in the amount of approximately $1,000 or $500 for students entering their 2nd year of studies.

(004) Ambassadorial Scholarships. The Rotary Foundation of Rotary International, One Rotary Center, 1560 Sherman Avenue, Evanston, IL 60201.

(005) Anthropology-Doctoral. Epilepsy Foundation of America, Behavioral Sciences Fellowships, Research Administration, 4351 Garden Ct Drive, Landover, MD.20785. (301) 459-3700. Criteria: Research that relates to epilepsy must be conducted. Deadline: March 1 each year.

(006) Anthropology-Graduate. Epilepsy Foundation of America, Behavioral Sciences Fellowships, Research Administration, 4351 Garden City Drive, Landover, MD 20785. (301) 459-3700.

Criteria: Research relating to epilepsy must be conducted. Deadline: March 1 each year.

(007) Anthropology-Undergraduate. Epilepsy Foundation of America, Behavioral Sciences Fellowships, Research Administration, 4351 Garden City Drive, Landover, MD 20785. (301) 459-3700.

Criteria: Research that relates to epilepsy must be conducted. Deadline: March 1 each year.

(008) Architecture-Graduate. The American Institute of Architects/The American Architectural Foundation Scholarship Programs,

The American Institute of Architects, 1735 New York Avenue, N. W., Washington, DC 20006-5292. Scholarship awards generally range from $1,000 to $2,500.

(009) Architecture-Undergraduate. The American Institute of Architects/The American Architectural Foundation Scholarship Programs, The American Institute of Architects, 1735 New York Avenue, N. W., Washington, DC 20006-5292. Scholarship awards generally range from $1,000 to $2,500.

(010) Armed Services-Air Force ROTC. To qualify, you must be a full-time student at a school offering Air Force ROTC, a U. S. citizen to receive a scholarship, be in good physical condition, have a good moral character and be at least 14 years old -17 to receive a scholarship appointment).

To qualify for this or the Professional Officer Course, please call the Air Force office in your city. Look in your phone directory.

(011) Armed Services-American Veterans-Graduate. AMVETS Scholarship Programs, 4647 Forbes Blvd., Lanham, MD 20706-4380, (301) 459-9600, Fax: (30l) 459 - 7924. For former members of the U. S. Armed Forces who have exhausted all government financial aid. You must be a United States of America citizen; demonstrate academic achievement; show financial need; and demonstrate involvement in extracurricular activities. Each year, one scholarship recipient receives $1,000.

(012) Armed Services-American Veterans Undergraduate. AMVETS National Scholarship, 4647 Forbes Blvd., Lanham, MD 20706-996l, (301) 459-9600, Fax: (30l) 459-7924. Criteria: (l) For children of veterans/former members of the U. S. Armed Forces (2) who have exhausted all federal government financial aid. (3) The recipient must have good grades (4) financial need. Each year, one scholarship recipient receive $1,000.

(013) Armed Services-Department of the Army. U. S. Army Health Professional Support Agency, The Curtis Center, Suite 460 West, Independence Square West, 60l Walnut Street, Philadelphia, PA 19102.

(014) Armed Services-Naval Academy. Director, Candidate Guidance, U. S. Naval Academy, ll7 Decatur Road, Annapolis, MD 21402-50l8, 1-800-638-9156. What is offered is a fully subsidized, four-year college education plus a monthly salary.

About 1,200 candidates are selected each year from nominations by the president and vice-president of the United States, the secretary of the Navy, U. S. senators and representatives.

A candidate must be a U. S. citizen, l7-2l years old, single, with no children. Naval Academy graduates must serve on active duty for at least 6 years as officers in the Navy or Marine Corps. Commencing in 1997, all newly commissioned officers will receive reserve commissions.

(015) Armed Services-Naval Reserve Officers Training Corps (NROTC). Navy-Marine Corps ROTC, College

COLLEGE: HOW TO GET THERE AND GO FREE
Scholarships Program, CDR Navy Recruiting Command Code 314, 801 North Randolph Street, Arlington, VA 22203-9705. 1 - 800 - USA -NAVY. This scholarship program is available to students who have graduated from high school before August 1 of the year they intend to start college.

There are 9 Steps required. (1) Preliminary application; (2) College Board score Release; (3) College application; (4) "Board-Eligible" Designation; (5) Scholarship Selection Board Application Processing; (6) Scholarship Selection Board Consideration; (7) Physical Qualification; (8) Travel; (9) Enrollment. "Thanks to you for your willingness to serve our country."

(016) Artistic Awards-Undergraduate. Scholarship Foundation of America, 55 Highway 35, Suite 5, Redbank, NJ 07701. Contact: Ellen Manning or Linda Paras. Awards average $1,000 for artistic merit..

(017) Broadcast Education. The National Association of Broadcast Education Association, Scholarships Program, 1771 N Street, N. W., Washington, DC 20036.

(018) Broadcast-Graduate. Broadcast Pioneers Scholarship, Broadcast Education Association, 1771 N Street, N. W., Washington, DC 20036-2891. (202) 429-5359. $1,250 grants are annually awarded. Deadline: January 15.

(019) Broadcast-Graduate. Dow Jones Newspaper Fund, P. O. Box 300, Princeton, NJ 08543-0300. (609) 452-2820. Forty-five internships are annually awarded $1,000 scholarships. Applications are available from October 1-November 1. Deadline: November 15.

(020) Broadcast-Undergraduate. Broadcast Pioneers Scholarship, Broadcast Education Association, 1771 N St. N. W., Washington, DC 20036-2891. (202) 429-5359. $1,250 grants are annually awarded. Deadline: January 15.

(021) Broadcast-Undergraduate. Dow Jones Newspaper Fund, P. O. Box 300, Princeton, NJ 08543-0300. (609) 452-2820. Forty-five internships are annually awarded, $1,000 scholarships. Applications are available from October to November 1. Deadline: November 15.

(022) Broadcasters. The National Association of Broadcasters, Scholarships Program, 1771 N Street, N. W., Washington, DC 20036

(023) Business-Doctorate. Applebaum Scholarships, The Food Distribution Research Society, P. O. Box 44110, Ft. Washington, MD 20749. Criterion: Applicants must have a sincere interest in the food industry. Grants awards are $500. Deadline: July 1 each year.

(024) Business-Graduate. Applebaum Scholarships, The Food Distribution Research Society, P. O. Box 44110, Ft. Washington, MD 20749. Criterion: Applicants must have a sincere interest in the food industry. Grants awards are $500. Deadline: July 1 each year.

(025) Business Technology. National Scholarships Trust Fund, 4615 Forbes Avenue, Pittsburgh, PA 15213. (412) 621-6941 Fax: (412) 621-3049. You must be pursuing an education as it has an application to the printing, publishing and packaging industries.

(026) Business-Undergraduate. Applebaum Scholarships, The Food Distribution Research Society, P. O. Box 44110, Ft. Washington, MD 20749. Criterion: Applicants must have a sincere interest in the food industry. Grants awards are $500. Deadline: July 1 each year.

(027) Chemistry-Graduate. National Scholarships Trust Fund, 4615 Forbes Avenue, Pittsburgh, PA 15213. (412) 621-6941 Fax: (412) 621-3049. You must be pursuing an education as it has an application to the printing, publishing and packaging industries.

(028) China Communications. Committee on Scholarly Communication With China, 1055 Thomas Jefferson Street, N. W., Suite 2013, Washington, DC 20007, (202) 337-1250 Fax: (202) 337-3109. Internet: China @ NAS.edu. TheDeadline is: October 15.

(029) Dance-Graduate. National Endowment For The Arts, Dance Program, Room 620, Nancy Hanks Center, 1100 Pennsylvania Avenue, N. W., Washington, DC 20506-0001. (202) 682-5435, (202) 682-5496, Voice/TT. They fund Choreographers, professional dance companies, organizations and individuals providing services to the field of dance.

(030) Dog Writers-Graduate. Dog Writers' Educational Trust Scholarship, P. O. Box 2220, Payson, AZ 85547-2220. (602) 474-8867. Applicants or close relatives must have past or present activities in dog shows, obedience or field trials. Each year, 5-10 $1,000 scholarships are available. A stamped, self-addressed envelope must accompany your request for an application. Deadline: December 31.

(031) Dog Writers-Undergraduate. Dog Writers' Educational Trust Scholarship, P. O. Box 2220, Payson, AZ 85547-2220. (602) 474-8867. Applicants or close relatives must have past or present activities in dog shows, obedience or field trials.

Each year, 5-10 $1,000 scholarships are available. A stamped, self-addressed envelope must accompany your request for an application. Deadline: December 31.

(032) Education Loans. Edith M. Strong Foundation, Loan Program, 1735 Eye Street, N. W., Suite 705, Washington, DC 20006.

(033) Education-Undergraduate. Maneely Fund, Inc., 900 Haddon Avenue., Suite 432, Collingswood, NJ 08108. Contact James E. O'Donnel, President. Initial contact is by writing a letter expressing your need for a grant and what you are plan to do after your graduation.

(034) Engineering-Undergraduate. National Scholarships Trust Fund, 4615 Forbes Avenue, Pittsburgh, PA 15213. (412) 621-6941 Fax: (412) 621-3049. You must be pursuing an education as it has an application to the printing, publishing and packaging industries. Washington, DC 20550.

(035) Ethnic-African American, Biology Doctorate.

National Science Foundation, 1800 G Street, N. W., Washington, DC 20550.

(036) Ethnic-African American, Biology Graduate. National Science Foundation, 1800 G Street, N. W., Washington, DC 20550.

(037) Ethnic-African American, Chemistry Doctorate. National Science Foundation, 1800 G Street, N. W., Washington, DC 20550.

(038) Ethnic-African American, Chemistry Graduate. National Science Foundation, 1800 G Street, N. W., Washington, DC 20550.

(039) Ethnic-African American, Computer Science. A T & T Bell Laboratories, Crawfords Corner Rd. Rm. 1E-213, Holmdel, NJ 07733-1988, (908)949-4301. Deadline: January 15 each year.

(040) Ethnic-African American, Energy Integrated Predoctoral. Fellowships are for manufacturing. U. S. Department of Energy Integrated Manufacturing, National Research Council, Office of Scientific and Engineering Personnel, 2101 Constitution Avenue, Washington, DC 20418, (202)334-2872. Deadline: November 4 each year.

(041) Ethnic-African American, Engineering. A T & T Bell Laboratories, Crawfords Corner Rd. Rm. 1E-213, Holmdel, NJ 07733-1988, (908)949-4301. Deadline: January 15 each year.

(042) Ethnic-African American, General. LULAC National Education Service Center, 777 N. Capital St., N.E.,Suite 305, Washington, DC 20002, (202)408-0060.

(043) Ethnic-African American, General. National Scholarship Service and Fund for Negro Students, 965 Martin Luther King, Jr. Drive, N. W., Atlanta, GA 30314 (404) 577-3990.

(044) Ethnic-African American, General. Director, Educational Services, 500 E. 62nd St., New York, NY 10021.

(045) Ethnic-African American, General. The Woodrow Wilson National Fellowship Foundation, 5 Vaughn Drive,

Suite 300, Princeton, NJ 08540-6313 (609) 452-7007, Fax. (609) 452-0066. Approximately 80 grants are awarded each year. Receives 1,000 applications annually. Grants are $12,500 plus tuition and fees. Deadline: December each year.

(046) Ethnic-African American, General Doctorate. Ford Foundation Dissertation Fellowship, New York, NY. Up to $8,800 for tuition, books, fees and reasonable living expenses. Maximum grant length is 36 months. Deadline: June 15 each year.

(047) Ethnic-African American, Biology Doctorate. National Science Foundation, 1800 G Street, N. W., Washington, DC 20550.

(048) Ethnic-African American, General Graduate. Patricia Roberts Harris Fellowships, ROB 3, Rm. 3022, 7th & D Streets, S. W., Washington, DC 20202-5251. Criterion: You must be enrolled in a graduate degree program that is under represented by women.

(049) Ethnic-African American, Geoscience. American Geological Institute, 4220 King Street, Alexandria, VA 22302-1507, (703) 379-2480, FAX: (703) 379-7563. You must be a United States citizen, a verifiable ethnic minority and a full-time student.

(050) Ethnic- African American, High School Students. Herbert Lehman Scholarships for African-American Students, 99 Hudson Street, New York, NY 10013, (212) 219-1900. This grant has existed since 1964 as a special project of students who have outstanding potential as evidenced by their high school academic records, test scores and personal essays. They must be of excellent character with strong recommendations from teachers, community representatives or employers. For more details, request an application after November 15 and before April 1, each year.

(051) Ethnic-African American, Internships. Office of Fellowships and Grants, Smithsonian Institution, Washington, DC 25060 (202) 287-3271, Internet: SIO

FG@SIVM.SI.EDU Request application materials by mail and allow at least 2 weeks for service in the continental U. S. to be made. Appointments carry at least a $250 weekly stipend.

(052) Ethnic-African American, Internships Engineering. University Corporation for Atmospheric Research, (NCAR) P. O. Box 3000, Boulder, CO 80307-3000, U.S., (303) 497-1650, Telex :989764, FAX: (303) 497-1654. NCAR is a federally supported non-profit laboratory for basic research in the atmospheric sciences. Grade Point Average (GPA) of 3.0 or better is expected.

Students must have completed their sophomore year of college, or the equivalent of two full-time years course work by June of this year and be an undergraduate.

The academic background of all applicants should include courses in at least one of the following areas of study: chemistry, biology, meteorology, physics, mathematics, computer science, electrical engineering, social science environmental issues or technical writing. Summer work internships begin approximately June 5 and end approximately August 11 of each year.

(053) Ethnic-African American, Journalism Graduate. National Association of Black Journalists, P. O. Box 17212, Washington, DC 20041, (703) 648-1270 Fax: (703) 476-6245. You must have completed at least one-full-semester of college to be eligible. For information about the $2,500 award, contact: Scholarship Coordinator at the above address.

(054) Ethnic-African American, Journalism Undergraduate. National Association of Black Journalists, P. O. Box 17212, Washington, DC 20041, (703) 648-1270   Fax: (703) 476-6245. You must have completed at least one, full-semester of college to be eligible. For information about the $2,500 award, contact: Scholarships for Ethnic Freshmen. Minority Affairs Director, ASNE, P. O. Box 17004, Washington, DC 20041. (703) 648-1146. Criteria: (1) Appli cants must have a 2.5 GPA in their high school courses (2) sign a statement of intent to pursue a college education with the intent of pursuing a career in journalism (3) submit a formal application form (4) two letters of recommendation (5) write an essay stating your career interests (6) have journalism-related activities while seniors in high school. Sixty $750 scholarships awarded. Criterion: You must be a third year medical student.

(055) Ethnic-African American, Journalism Undergraduate. National Newspaper Publishers Association Grants, Chairman, NNPA Scholarship Committee, 948 National Press Building, Washington, DC 20045. Offers 10 grants valued at $2,000 each annually awarded.

(056) Ethnic-African American, Journalism Undergraduate. American Society of Newspaper Editors Foundation Scholarships for Ethnic Freshmen. Minority Affairs Director, ASNE, P. O. Box 17004, Washington, DC 20041, (703) 648-1146. Criteria: (1) Applicants must have a 2.5 GPA in their high school courses (2) sign a statement of intent to pursue a college education with the intent of pursuing a career in journalism (3) submit a formal application form (4) two letters of recommendation (5) write an essay stating your career interests (6) have journalism-related activities while seniors in high school. Sixty $750 scholarships awarded.

(057) Ethnic-African American, Law Research Undergraduate. American Bar Foundation, 750 N. Lake Shore Drive, Chicago, I1058) Ethnic-African American, Mathematics Doctorate . National Science Foundation, 1800 G Street, N. W., Washington, DC 20550.

(058) Ethnic-African American, Mathematics Doctorate. National Science Foundation, 1800 G Street, N. W., Washington, DC 20550.

(059) Ethnic-African American, Mathematics Graduate. National Science Foundation, 1800 G Street, N. W., Washington, DC 20550.

(060) Ethnic-African American, Medical. National Medical Fellowships, Inc., 254 W. 31st Street, 7th Fl., New York, NY 10001.Criterion:You must be a 3rd yr. medical student.

(061) Ethnic-African American, Nursing. Frances Tomkins General Scholarships, The Foundation of the National Student Nurses' Association, Inc. 555 W. 57th Street, Suite 1325, New York, NY 10019. (212) 581-2215. Awards are $1,000-$2,500. Deadline: February 1.

(062) Ethnic-African American, Political Science Graduate. The American Political Science Association, Ethnic Graduate Fellowship Program, 1527 New Hampshire Avenue, N. W., Washington, DC 20036. (202) 483-2512, Fax: (202) 483-2657.

You must enroll in a doctoral program in the United States of America. Applicants may have mixed social science undergraduate majors. You must have success in graduate studies. Fifteen fellowship grants of $8,000 for one year of study.

(063) Ethnic-African American, Religion Episcopal. Evangelical Education Society, 2300 9th Street S., Suite 301, Arlington, VA 22204-2351. (703) 521-3264. For theological studies. Grants awards are $500-$1,000 each year.

(064) Ethnic-African American, Religion Methodists. Scholarship Committee, United Methodist Communications, Public Media Division, P. O. Box 320, Nashville, TN 37202. Recipients must show commitment and involvement in the life of the church.

Clarity of purpose in the plans and goals for the future. You must show potential professional usefulness as a religious journalist. Scholarships are for $2,500.

(065) Ethnic-African American, Science. Ethnic Access to Research Careers, Biomedical Research, Public Health Service, National Institutes of Health, National Institute of General Medical Sciences, Bethesda, Maryland 20892.

(066) Ethnic-African American, Science Doctorate. National Science Foundation, 1800 G Street, N. W., Washington, DC 20550.

(067) Ethnic-African American, Science Graduate. National Science Foundation, 1800 G Street, N. W., Washington, DC 20550.

(068) Ethnic-African American, Science Post-doctoral. National Research Council, Office of Scientific and Engineering Personnel, 2101 Constitution Avenue, Washington, D C 20418, (202) 334-2872, Ford Foundation pre-doctoral and dissertation fellowships are due November 4, each year.

(069) Ethnic-African American, Science Pre-doctoral. National Research Council, Office of Scientific and Engineering Personnel, 2101 Constitution Avenue, Washington, DC 20418, (202) 334-2872.

Ford Foundation pre-doctoral and dissertation fellowships are due November 4, each year.

(070) Ethnic-African American, Social Science. The American Political Science Association, Ethnic Graduate Fellowship Program, 1527 New Hampshire Avenue, N. W., Washington, DC 20036.

You must enroll in a doctoral program in the United States of America. Applicants may have mixed social science undergraduate majors.

You must have success in graduate studies. Fifteen fellowship grants of $8,000 are annually provided for one year of study.

(071) Ethnic-African American, Social Science. Maneely Fund, Inc., 900 Haddon Avenue., Suite 432, Collingswood, NJ 08108. Contact James E. O'Donnel, President.

Initial contact is by writing a letter expressing your need for a grant and what you plan to do after your graduation.

(072) Ethnic-African American, Social Science Graduate.

The American Political Science Association, Ethnic Graduate Fellowship Program, 1527 New Hampshire Avenue, N. W., Washington, DC 20036, You must enroll in a doctoral program in the United States of America. Applicants may have mixed social science undergraduate majors. You must have completed one year of study. Apply prior to December 1, of the year before enrollment.

(073) Ethnic-African American, Social Science Research Undergraduate. American Bar Foundation, 750 N. Lake ShoreDrive, Chicago, IL 60611. You must be a United States Citizen. Awards are 10-weeks stipends for $3,300.

(074) Ethnic-African American, Social Work Graduate. American Cancer Society Clinical Oncology, 1599 Clifton Road, N. E., Atlanta, GA. (404) 329-5734 Fax: (404) 325-1467. Recipients will support hospital-based training. Deadline: October 1.

(075) Ethnic-African American, Social Work Males. Heath Educational Fund. c/o First Florida Bank, N. A., P. O. Box 11311, St. Petersburg, FL 33713. Grantor gives 10 grants of $500 each. Deadline: Varies.

(076) Ethnic-African American, Social Work Post-Graduate. American Cancer Society Clinical Oncology, 1599 Clifton Road, N. E., Atlanta, GA. (404) 329-5734 Fax: (404) 325-1467. Recipients will support hospital-based training. Deadline: October 1.

(077) Ethnic-African American, Sociology Doctorate. American Sociological Association Research Doctoral Fellowships in Sociology, 1722 N. Street, N.W., Washington, DC 20036. (202) 883-3410, Fax: (202) 785-0146. Fifteen fellowships of $8,000. Deadline: December 31.

(078) Ethnic-African American, Technology Doctorate. National Science Foundation, 1800 G Street, N. W., Washington, DC 20550.

(079) Ethnic-African American, Technology Graduate. National Science Foundation, 1800 G Street, N. W., Wash ington, DC 20550.

(080) Ethnic-Alaska Native, General Alaska Native Brotherhood/ Sisterhood, 318 Wiloughby Street, Juneau, AK 99801, (907) 586-2219. Amounts vary. Grant duration is for approximately 4 years. Deadline: varies.

(081) Ethnic-Alaska Native, General Department of Health & Human Services, Public Health Service, Aberdeen Area, Indian Health Service, Federal Building, Room 309, Aberdeen, SD 57401. (605) 226-7553.

This program provides financial assistance for students only to enroll in courses that will prepare them for acceptance into health professions, schools, i. e., medicine, nursing, dentistry, etc. Courses may be either compensatory (required to improve science, mathematics, or other basic skills and knowledge) or professional (required in order to qualify for admission into a health professions program).

Priority is given to Graduate Students, and junior and senior level students, unless otherwise specified

(082) Ethnic-Alaska Native, Teacher/Education Undergraduate. Alaska Program for Native Students, Financial Aid Office, University of Fairbanks, AK 99775 (312) 943-9090. Grants awards are $1,000 each. Deadline: varies.

(083) Ethnic-Asian American, Journalism Undergraduate. Asian American Journalists Association, 1765 Sutter Street, Rm. 1000, San Francisco, CA 94115. Ethnic Media Internships are awarded with $1,500 stipends. Deadline: November 1 each year.

(084) Ethnic-Asian (Southeast), Refugees. Phillips Brooks House Association, Inc., Harvard University, Cambridge, MA 02138-6533, (617)495-5526, FAX: (617)496-2461. Deadline: November 16, each year.

(085) Ethnic-Asian, Social Science. The American Political Science Association, Ethnic Graduate Fellowship Program, 1527 New Hampshire Avenue, N. W., Washington, DC 20036. You must enroll in a doctoral program in the

United States of America. Applicants may have mixed social science undergraduate majors. You must have success
in graduate studies. Fifteen fellowship grants of $8,000
for one year of study.

(086) Ethnic-Asian, Sociology Doctorate. American Sociological Association Research Doctoral Fellowships in Sociology, 1722 N. Street, N.W., Washington, DC 20036. (202)
883-3410, Fax: (202) 785-0146. Fifteen fellowships of $8,000.
Deadline: December 31.

**(087) Ethnic-Canadian, Fellowship Pre-doctoral, Post-doc-
toral.** American Institute of Pakistan Studies, P. O. Box 7568,
Wake Forest University, Winston-Salem, NC 27109, (919) 759-
5453/5449 Fax: (919) 759-6104.

(088) Ethnic-Canadian, Social Sciences Doctorate. Harry
Frank Guggenheim Foundation, 90 Park Avenue, New
York, N Y 10016. (212)687-4470.

You must be at your dissertation level. Grants awards
are based upon individual needs and the recipients' resources. Deadline: October 1 each year.

(089) Ethnic-Caribbean, Social Sciences Doctorate. Harry
Frank Guggenheim Foundation, 90 Park Avenue, New
York, NY 10016. (212) 687-4470.

You must be at your dissertation level. Grants awards
are based upon individual needs and the recipients' resources. Deadline: October 1 each year.

(090) Ethnic-Hispanic, Actuarial Science. Society of Actuaries, 475 N. Martingale Road, Suite 800, Schaumburg,
IL 60173 (708) 706-3500. Provides a scholarship program
via Casualty Actuarial Society and Society of Actuaries.

(091) Ethnic-Hispanic, Biology Doctorate. National Science
Foundation, 1800 G Street, N. W., Washington, DC 20550.

(092) Ethnic-Hispanic, Biology Graduate. National Science
Foundation, 1800 G Street, N. W., Washington, DC 20550.

(093) Ethnic-Hispanic, Chemistry Graduate. National Science Foundation, 1800 G Street, N. W., Washington, DC

20550.

(094) Ethnic-Hispanic, Chemistry Doctorate. National Science Foundation, 1800 G Street, N. W., Washington, DC 20550.

(095) Ethnic-Hispanic, Computer Science. A T & T Bell Laboratories, Crawfords Corner Rd. Rm. 1E-213, Holmdel, NJ 07733-1988, (908)949-4301. Deadline: January 15 each year.

(096) Ethnic-Hispanic, Energy Integrated Pre-doctoral. Fellowships are for manufacturing. U. S. Department of Energy Integrated Manufacturing, National Research Council, Office of Scientific and Engineering Personnel, 2101 Constitution Avenue, Washington, DC 20418, (202)334-2872. Deadline: November 4 each year.

(097) Ethnic-Hispanic, Engineering. A T & T Bell Laboratories, Crawfords Corner Rd. Rm. 1E-213, Holmdel, NJ 07733-1988, (908)949-4301. Deadline: January 15 each year.

(098) Ethnic-Hispanic, General. National Hispanic Scholarship Fund, P. O. Box 728, Novato, Calif. 94948.

(099) Ethnic-Hispanic, General. LULAC National Education Service Center, 777 N. Capital St., N. E., Suite 305, Washington, DC 20002, (202)408-0060

(100) Ethnic-Hispanic, General. Hispanic Public Relations Association, of Los Angeles California, Los Angeles, California. Scholarships averaging $1,000 .

(101) Ethnic-Hispanic, General. The Woodrow Wilson National Fellowship Foundation, 5 Vaughn Drive, Suite 300, Princeton, NJ 0540-6313 (609) 452-7007, Fax. (609) 452-0066. Deadline: December each year.

(102) Ethnic-Hispanic, General Doctorate. Ford Foundation Dissertation Fellowship, New York, NY. Up to $8,-000 for tuition, books, fees and reasonable living expenses. Maximum grant length is 36 months. Deadline June 1

(103) Ethnic-Hispanic, Geophysics. The American Political Science Association, Ethnic Graduate Fellowship Pro gram, 1527 New Hampshire Avenue, N. W., Washington, DC 20036. Fifteen fellowship grants of $8,000 be enrolled in a graduate degree program that is under-represented by women. The fund for these awards is $21, 780,000. Deadline: Varies

(104) Ethnic-Hispanic, Geoscience. American Geological Institute, 4220 King Street, Alexandria, VA 22302-1507, (703) 379-2480, FAX: (703) 379-7563. You must be a U.S. Citizen.

(105) Ethnic-Hispanic, Internships Engineering. University Corporation for Atmospheric Research, (NCAR) P. O. Box 3000, Boulder, CO 80307-3000, U.S., (303) 497-1650, Telex :989764, FAX: (303) 497-1654. NCAR is a federally supported non-profit laboratory for basic research in the atmospheric sciences.

Students must have completed their sophomore year of college, or the equivalent of two full-time years course work by June of this year.

You must have a cumulative GPA of 3.0 or better, and be an undergraduate. The academic background of all applicants should include courses in at least one of the following areas of study: chemistry, biology, meteorology, physics, mathematics, computer science, electrical engineering, social science, environmental issues or technical writing. Summer work internships begin approximately June 5 and end approximately August 11, each year.

(106) Ethnic-Hispanic, Journalism Broadcast Graduate Students. National Association of Hispanic Journalists, 1193 National Press Building, Washington, DC 20045. Awards are $1,000. Deadline: January 31 each year.

(107) Ethnic-Hispanic, Journalism Broadcast Undergraduate High School Students. National Association of Hispanic Journalists, 1193 National Press Building, Washington, DC 20045. Awards are $1,000. Deadline: January 31, each year.

(108) Ethnic-Hispanic, Journalism Broadcast Undergradu

ate. National Association of Hispanic Journalists, 1193 National Press Building Suite 1193, Washington, DC 20045. Awards are $1,000. Deadline: January 31, each year.

(109) Ethnic-Hispanic, Journalism Print High School Students National Association of Hispanic Journalists, 1193 National Press Building, Washington, DC 20045. Awards are $1,000. Deadline: January 31 each year.

(110) Ethnic-Hispanic, Journalism Print Graduate National Association of Hispanic Journalists, 1193 National Press Building, Washington, DC 20045. Awards are $1,000. Deadline: January 31, each year.

(111) Ethnic-Hispanic, Journalism Print Undergraduate. National Association of Hispanic Journalists, 1193 National Press Building Suite 1193, Washington, DC 20045. Awards are $1,000. Deadline: January 31 each year.

(112) Ethnic-Hispanic, Law Research Undergraduate. American Bar Foundation, 750 N. Lake Shore Drive, Chicago, IL 60611. You must be a United States Citizen.

(113) Ethnic-Hispanic, Mathematics Doctorate. National Science Foundation, 1800 G Street, N. W., Washington, DC 20550.

(114) Ethnic-Hispanic, Mathematics Graduate. National Science Foundation, 1800 G Street, N. W., Washington, DC 20550.

(115) Ethnic-Hispanic, Medical. National Medical Fellowships, Inc., 254 W. 31st Street, 7th Fl., New York, NY 10001. Criterion: You must be a third year medical student.

(116) Ethnic-Hispanic, Political Science Graduate. The American Political Science Association, Ethnic Graduate Fellowship Program, 1527 New Hampshire Avenue, NW Washington, DC 20036. (202) 483-2512. Fax: (202)483-2657.**(117) Ethnic-Hispanic, Science Doctorate.** National Science Foundation, 1800 G Street, N. W., Washington, D C 20550.

(118) Ethnic-Hispanic, Science Graduate. National Science Foundation, 1800 G S Street, N. W., Washington, D C 20550. Criteria: (1) a college level student. (2) at least one parent must be of Italian extraction and (4) you must have a "B" average or better.

(119) Ethnic-Hispanic, Science Post-doctoral. National Research Council, Office of Scientific and Engineering Personnel, 2101 Constitution Avenue, Washington, DC 20418, (202) 334-2872, Ford Foundation pre-doctoral and dissertation fellowships are due November 4, of each year.

(120) Ethnic-Hispanic, Science Pre-doctoral. National Research Council, Office of Scientific and Engineering Personnel, 2101 Constitution Avenue, Washington, DC 20418, (202) 334-2872, Ford Foundation pre-doctoral and dissertation fellowships are due November 4, of each year.

(121) Ethnic-Hispanic, Social Science. The American Political Science Association, Ethnic Graduate Fellowship Program, 1527 New Hampshire Avenue, N. W., Washington, DC 20036.

You must enroll in a doctoral program in the United States of America. Applicants may have mixed social science undergraduate majors.

You must have success in graduate studies. Fifteen fellowship grants of $8,000 for one year of study.

(122) Ethnic-Hispanic, Social Science. Maneely Fund, Inc., 900 Haddon Avenue., Suite 432, Collingswood, NJ 08108. Contact James E. O'Donnel, President. Initial contact is by writing a letter expressing your need for a grant and what you plan to do after your graduation.

(123) Ethnic-Hispanic, Social Science Doctorate. Harry Frank Guggenheim Foundation, 90 Park Avenue, New York, NY 10016. (212) 687-4470.

You must be at your dissertation level. Grants awards are based upon individual needs and the recipients' resources. Deadline: October 1 each year.

(124) Ethnic-Hispanic, Social Science Research Under

graduate. American Bar Foundation, 750 N. Lake Shore Drive, Chicago, IL 60611.

You must be a United States of America Citizen. Awards are 10-weeks stipends for $3,300.

(125) Ethnic-Hispanic, Social Work Graduate. American Cancer Society Clinical Oncology, 1599 Clifton Road, N. E., Atlanta, GA. (404) 329-5734 Fax: (404) 325-1467.

Recipients will support hospital-based training. Deadline: October 1.

(126) Ethnic-Hispanic, Social Work Males. Heath Educational Fund. c/o First Florida Bank, N. A., P. O. Box 11311, St. Petersburg, FL 33713.

Grantor gives 10 grants of $500 each. Deadline: Varies.

(127) Ethnic-Hispanic, Social Work Post-Graduate. American Cancer Society Clinical Oncology, 1599 Clifton Road, N. E., Atlanta, GA. (404) 329 - 5734 Fax: (404) 325-1467.

Recipients will support hospital-based training.

(128) Ethnic-Hispanic, Sociology Doctorate. American Sociological Association Research Doctoral Fellowships in Sociology, 1722 N. Street, N.W., Washington, DC 20036. (202) 883-3410, Fax: (202) 785-0146.

Fifteen fellowships $8,000 each are awarded. Deadline: December 31 each year.

(129) Ethnic-Hispanic, Technology Doctorate. National Science Foundation, 1800 G Street, N. W., Washington, DC 20550.

(130) Ethnic-Hispanic, Technology Graduate. National Science Foundation, 1800 G Street, N. W., Washington, DC 20550.

(131) Ethnic-Italian, Communications Graduate The John Fischetti Scholarship Award Executive Director, Scholarship Fund, 2911 N. W. 39th Street, Miami, FL 33142 or call (305)634-2465. Presented annually by the Joint Civic Committee of Italian Americans, and it is given to: (l) students who are undergraduate seniors accepted into a graduate program. (2) a college level student (3) at least one parent must be of Italian extraction and (4) you must have a "B" average or better.

(132) Ethnic-Italian, Communications Undergraduate. The John Fischetti Scholarship Award. Executive Director, Scholarship Fund, 29ll NW 39th Street, Miami, FL 33l42 or call (305) 634-2465. Presented annually by the Joint Civic Committee of Italian Americans, and it is given to: (l) students who are high school seniors accepted into a college program (2) a college level student. (3) at least one parent must be of Italian extraction and (4) you must have a "B" average or better.

(133) Ethnic-Italian, General Graduate. Sons of Italy Foundation, 2l9 E Street, NE, Washington, DC 20002. 202) 547-2900. For people of Italian descent and full-time students at accredited universities. Annually, fourteen awards of $2,000 each are made.

(134) Ethnic-Italian General Undergraduate. Sons of Italy Foundation, 2l9 E Street, NE, Washington, DC 20002. (202) 547-2900. For people of Italian descent and full-time students at accredited universities. Annually, fourteen awards of $2,000 each are made.

(135) Ethnic-Italian, Journalism Graduate. The John Fischetti Scholarship Award. Executive Director, Scholarship Fund, 29ll NW 39th Street, Miami, FL 33l42. Or call (305) 634-2465. Presented annually by the Joint Civic Committee of Italian Americans, and it is given to (l) students who are undergraduate senior s accepted into a graduate program (2) a college level student (3) at least one parent must be of Italian extraction and (4) you must have a "B" average or better.

(136) Ethnic-Italian, Journalism Undergraduate. The John Fichetti Scholarship Award. Executive Director, Scholar ship Fund, 2911 NW 39th Street, Miami, FL 33142. Or call (305) 634-2465. Presented annually by the Joint Civic Committee of Italian Americans, and it is given to (1) students who are high school seniors accepted into a college program (2) a college level student. (3) at least one parent must be of Italian extraction and (4) you must have a "B"average or better.

(137) Ethnic-Japanese, Graduate. The Japan Foundation, 152 West 57th Street, 39th. Floor, New York, NY 10019.

(138) Ethnic-Japanese, Undergraduate. The Japan Foundation, 152 West 57th Street, 39th. Floor, New York, NY 10019.

(139) Ethnic-Jewish Affairs. The JDC-Smolar Student Journalism Award, Joint Distribution Committee, 711 Third Avenue, New York, NY 10017, ATTN: Amirf Shaviv.

Applicants must submit an article or story written or translated into English which promotes an understanding of overseas needs.

Submissions must be published in a newspaper and/ or magazine which are substantially involved in the coverage of Jewish affairs. This $1,000 award is annual. by the American Jewish Joint Distribution Committee.

(140) Ethnic-Jewish Studies. Memorial Foundation for Jewish Culture, International Doctoral Scholarships for Studies Specializing in Jewish Fields , 15 E. 26th Street, New York, NY 10010. (212) 679-4074. Criteria: You must be officially enrolled in a doctoral program at a recognized university.

(141) Ethnic-Native American Indian, Actuarial Science. Graduate. Society of Actuaries, 475 N. Martingale Road, Suite 800, Schaumburg, IL

(142) Ethnic-Native American Indian, Actuarial Science. Undergraduate. Society of Actuaries, 475 N. Martingale Road, Suite 800, Schaumburg, IL. Provides a scholarship program via Casualty Actuarial Society and of Actuaries.

(143) Ethnic-Native American Indian, Arts. Arts Schol

arship P. O. Box 20007, Santa Fe, NM 87504..

(144) Ethnic-Native American Indian, Biology Doctorate. National Science Foundation, 1800 G Street, N. W., Wash-ington, DC 20550.

(145) Ethnic-Native American Indian, Business Administration Undergraduate. Fellowships For Indian Students, Office of Indian Education, Elementary and Secondary Education, Department of Education. Contact: Indian Fellowship Program, 400 Maryland Avenue, S. W., Washington, DC 20550.

For an individual who: (1) is a member of a tribe, band, or other organized group of Indians including those tribes, bands or groups terminated since 1940 and those recognized by the State in which they reside; (2) is a descendant in the first or second degree of any individual described above, or (3) is considered by the Secretary of the Interior to be an Indian for any purpose; or (4) is an Eskimo, Aleut, or other Alaska Native; United States citizen.

Also,, is in attendance, or who has been accepted for admission, as a full-time graduate or in an eligible field of study at an accredited institution of higher education and recognized as a degree candidate may apply. An applicant must not have obtained a terminal degree.

(146) Ethnic-Native American Indian, Chemistry Doctorate. National Science Foundation, 1800 G Street, N. W., Washington, DC 20550.

(147) Ethnic-Native American Indian, Chemistry Graduate. National Science Foundation, 1800 G Street, N.W., Washington, DC 20550.

(148) Ethnic-Native American Indian, Chemistry Doctorate. National Science Foundation, 1800 G Street, N. W., Washington, DC 20550.

(149) Ethnic-Native American Indian, Chemistry Graduate. National Science Foundation, 1800 G Street, N. W., Washington, DC 20550.

(150) Ethnic-Native American Indian, Computer Science. A T & T Bell Laboratories, Crawfords Corner Rd. Rm. 1E-213, Holmdel, NJ 07733-1988, (908) 949-4301.

Deadline: January 15 each year. Department of Education. Contact: Indian Fellowship 20202-5249.

(151) Ethnic-Native American Indian, Education Undergraduate. Contact: Indian Fellowship Program, 400 Maryland Avenue, S. W., Washington, DC 20202-5249.

(152) Ethnic-Native American Indian, Education Graduate. Contact: Indian Fellowship Program, 400 Maryland Avenue, S. W., Washington, DC 20202-5249.

(153) Ethnic-Native American Indian, Energy Integrated Pre-doctoral. Fellowships are for manufacturing. U. S. Department of Energy Integrated Manufacturing, National Research Council, (202) 334-2872. Deadline: November 4.

(154) Ethnic-Native American Indian, Engineering Undergraduate. Fellowships For Indian Students, Office 1, Office of Scientific and Engineering Personnel, 2101 Constitution Avenue, Washington, DC 20418, (202) 334-2872. Deadline: November 4 each year.

(155) Ethnic-Native American Indian, Engineering Undergraduate. A T & T Bell Laboratories, Crawfords Corner Rd. Rm. 1E-213, Holmdel, NJ 07733-1988, (908) 949-4301. Deadline: January 15 each year.

(156) Ethnic-Native American Indian, Engineering Undergraduate. A T & T Bell Laboratories, Crawfords Corner Rd. Rm. 1E-213, Holmdel, NJ 07733-1988, (908) 949-4301. Deadline: January 15 each year.

(157) Ethnic-Native American Indian, Fellowships Psychology. Office of Indian Education, Elementary and Secondary Education, Department of Education.

Contact: I. F. P., 400 Maryland Avenue, S. W., Washington, DC 20202-5249. You must annually reapply.

(158) Ethnic-Native American Indian, General Graduate. Patricia Roberts Harris Fellowships, ROB 3, Rm. 3022, 7th

& D Streets, S. W., Washington, DC 20202 -5251. Criterion: You must be enrolled in a graduate degree program that is under-represented by women. The fund for these awards is $21, 780,000. Deadline: Varies

(159) Ethnic-Native American Indian, General Graduate. American Indian Graduate Center, 4520 Montgomery Blvd., N E, Suite 1-B, Albuquerque, NM 87109 (505) 881-4584. Grants awards up to $4,000 annually. Deadline: April 30.

(160) Ethnic-Native American Indian, General Undergraduate. The Higher Education Grant Program provides grants to Indian students to work toward an undergraduate degree. Students must apply and gain admission to an accredited college or university. Last year, over 14,800 students were provided grants. For further information, call Garry Martin at (202) 208-4871.

(161) Ethnic-Native American Indian, General Undergraduate. American Indian Development Foundation, AISES, Scholarship, 1630 30th St., Suite 301, Boulder, CO 80301-1014 (302) 492-8658, Grants awards are $1,000 a year. You must annually reapply.

(162) Ethnic-Native American Indian, General Undergraduate. International Order Of The King's Daughters & Sons, North American Indian Department, 5451 Cameo Court, Pleasanton, CA 94588 (510) 847-0105. Average Grant is $500 Deadline: April 15.

163) Ethnic-Native American Indian, General Undergraduate. American Indian Development Foundation, AISES, Scholarship, 1630 30th St., Suite 301, Boulder, CO 80301-1014 (302) 492-8658, Grants awards are $1,000 a year.

(164) Ethnic-Native American Indian, Geoscience. American Geological Institute, 4220 King Street, Alexandria, VA 22302-1507, (703) 379-2480, FAX: (703) 379-7563. You must be a United States citizen, a verifiable ethnic minority and a full-time student.

(165) Ethnic-Native American Indian, Internships. Office

85

of Fellowships and Grants, Smithsonian Institution, Washington, DC 25060(202) 287-3271, Internet: SIOFG@SIVM.SI.EDU Request application materials by mail and allow at least 2 weeks for service in the continental U. S. to be made. Appointments carry at least a $250 weekly stipend.

(166) Ethnic-Native American Indian, Internships Engineering. University Corporation for Atmospheric Research, (NCAR) P. O. Box 3000, Boulder, CO 80307-3000, U.S., (303) 497-1650, Telex: 989764, FAX: (303) 497-1654. NCAR is a federally supported non-profit laboratory for basic research in the atmospheric sciences.

Students must have completed their sophomore year of college, or the equivalent of two full-time years course work by June of this year. You must have a cumulative GPA of 3.0 or better, and be an undergraduate.

The academic background of all applicants should include courses in at least one of the following areas of study: chemistry, biology, meteorology, physics, mathematics, computer science, electrical engineering, social science or environmental issues or technical writing.

Summer work internships begin approximately June 5 and end approximately August 11 each year.

(167) Ethnic-Native American Indian, Law. Graduate Fellowships For Indian Students, Office of Indian Education, Elementary and Secondary Education, Department of Education. Contact: Indian Fellowship Shore Drive, Chicago, IL 60611.

You must be a United States of America Citizen. Awards are 10-weeks stipends for $3,300.

(168) Ethnic-Native American Indian, General Graduate. American Indian Development Foundation, AISES, Scholarship, 1630-30th St., Suite 301, Boulder, CO   803-01-1014 (302) 492-8658, Grants awards are $1,000 a year. You must annually apply.

(169) Ethnic-Native American Indian, Mathematics Doctorate. National Science Foundation, 1800 G Street, N. W., Washington, DC 20550.

(170) Ethnic-Native American Indian, Mathematics Graduate. National Science Foundation, 1800 G Street, N. W., Washington, DC 20550.

(171) Ethnic-Native American Indian, Medical. National Medical Fellowships, Inc., 254 W. 31st Street, 7th Fl., New York, NY 10001. Criterion: You must be a third year medical student.

(172) Ethnic-Native American Indian Medicine Graduate. Fellowships For Indian Students, Office of Indian Education, Elementary and Secondary Education, Department of Education. Contact: Indian Fellowship Program, 400 Maryland Avenue, S. W., Washington, DC 20202-5249.

(173) Ethnic-Native American Indian Preparatory. Department of Health & Human Services, Public Health Service, Aberdeen Area, Indian Health Service, Federal Building, Room 309, Aberdeen, SC 57401 (605)226-7553.

This program provides financial assistance for students only to enroll in courses that will prepare them for acceptance into health professions, schools, i. e., medicine, nursing, dentistry, etc.

Courses may be either compensatory (required to improve science, mathematics, or other basic skills and knowledge) or professional (required in order to qualify for admission into a health professions program). Priority is given to Graduate Students, junior and senior level students, unless otherwise specified.

(174) Ethnic-Native American Indian, Science Doctorate. National Science Foundation, 1800 G Street, N. W., Washington, DC 20550.

(175) Ethnic-Native American Indian, Science Graduate. National Science Foundation, 1800 G Street, N. W., Washington, DC 20550

(176) Ethnic-Native American Indian, Science Post-doctoral. National Research Council, Office of Scientific and Engineering Personnel, 2101 Constitution Avenue, Washington, DC 20418, (202) 334-2872, Ford Foundation pre-doctoral and dissertation fellowships are due November 4, each year.

(177) Ethnic-Native American Indian, Science Pre-doctoral. National Research Council, Office of Scientific and Engineering Personnel, 2101 Constitution Avenue, Washington, DC 20418, (202) 334-2872, Ford Foundation pre-doctoral and dissertation fellowships are due November 4, each year.

(178) Ethnic-Native American Indian, Social Science. The American Political Science Association, Ethnic Graduate Fellowship Program, 1527 New Hampshire Avenue, N. W., Washington, DC 20036. You must enroll in a doctoral program in the United States of America. Applicants may have mixed social science undergraduate majors. You must have success in graduates studies. Fifteen fellowship grants of $8,000 for one year of study.

(179) Ethnic-Native American Indian, Social Science. Maneely Fund, Inc., 900 Haddon Avenue, Suite 432, Collingswood, NJ 08108. Contact James E. O'Donnel,

(180) Ethnic-Native American Indian, Social Science Doctorate. American Sociological Association Research 1722 N. Street, N.. W., Washington, DC 20036. (202) 883-3410, Fax: (202) 785-0146. Initial contact is by writing a letter expressing your need for a grant and what you plan to do after your graduation. Deadline: December 31.

(181) Ethnic-Native American Indian, Social Science Undergraduate. American Bar Foundation, 750 N. Lake Shore Drive, Chicago, IL 60611. You must be a United States of America Citizen. Awards are 10-weeks stipends for $3,300.

(182) Ethnic-Native American Indian, Social Work Graduate. American Cancer Society Clinical Oncology, 1599

Clifton Road, N. E., Atlanta, GA. (404) 329-5734 Fax: (404) 325-1467. Recipients will support hospital-based training. Deadline: October 1.

(183) Ethnic-Native American Indian, Social Work Males. Heath Educational Fund. c/o First Florida Bank, N. A. P. O. Box 11311, St. Petersburg, FL 33713. Grantor gives 10 grants of $500 each. Deadline: Varies.

(184) Ethnic-Native American Indian, Social Work Post-Graduate. American Cancer Society Clinical Oncology, 1599 Clifton Road, N. E., Atlanta, GA. (404) 329-5734 Fax: (404) 325-1467. Recipients will support hospital-based training. Deadline: October 1.

(185) Ethnic-Native American Indian, Technology Doctorate. National Science Foundation, 1800 G Street, N. W., Washington, DC 20550.

(186) Ethnic-Native American Indian, Technology Graduate. National Science Foundation, 1800 G Street, N. W. Washington, DC 20550.

(187) Ethnic-Native American Indian, Technology Doctorate. National Science Foundation, 1800 G Street, N. W. Washington, DC 20550.

(188) Ethnic-Native American Indian, Technology Graduate. National Science Foundation, 1800 G Street, N. W. Washington, DC 20550.

(189) Ethnic-Polish, Graduate. Kosciuszko Foundation Year Abroad at Universities in Poland Scholarships, 15 East 65th Street, New York, NY 10021-6595. For United States students who possess a knowledge of the Polish Language.

Grants will pay tuition, housing and a monthly stipend for living expenses. Transportation to and from Poland is at the recipients' expense. A $50 non-refundable fee must accompany your application.

(190) Ethnic-Polish, Post-Graduate. Kosciuszko Foundation Year Abroad at Universities in Poland Scholarships, 15 East 65th Street, New York, NY 10021-6595. For United States students who possess a knowledge of the Polish Language.

Grants will pay tuition, housing and a monthly stipend for living expenses. Transportation to and from Poland is at the recipients' expense. A $50 non-refundable fee must accompany your application.

Federal Grant Eligibility. Eligibility for federal grants require your being enrolled at least half - time, and you must meet the usual student aid minimum requirements for matriculation by obtaining C -level grades. Halftime means at least 6 semester hours or quarter hours per term.

Federal HOPE Scholarship. This is not a scholarship but a tax-credit, the HOPE legislation allows eligible students pursuing the first two years of post-secondary education to receive a tax credit for 100 percent of the first $1,000 of tuition and fees and 50 percent of the second $1,000 on their federal income tax.

Students must be enrolled at least halftime (6-credit hours) in a degree, certificate or other program leading to matriculation.

(191) Federal Pell Grants. Federal Student Financial Aid Information Center 1 (800) 433-3243, TD (line for hearing impaired people) 1 (800) 730-8913. Criteria: (1) Recipients must demonstrate financial need; (2) be enrolled or accepted for enrollment at an approved institution; (3) be enrolled at least halftime; (4) not owe a refund on any grant; (5) be in default on any loan; (6) be a U. S. citizen or eligible noncitizen; (7) sign an Anti-Drug Abuse Act Certification (8) a listing of all the additional details about Federal Government sponsored programs is available from Federal Student Aid Information Center, P. O. Box 84, Washington, DC, 20044.

(192) Federal Supplemental Educational Opportunity Grants (FSEOG). Federal Student Financial Aid Information Center 1 (800) 433-3243, TDD (line for hearing impaired people) 1 (800) 730-8913. Criteria: (1) Recipients must demonstrate exceptional financial need; (2) be enrolled or accepted for enrollment at an approved institution; (3) be enrolled at least halftime; (4) not owe a refund on any grant; (5) be in default on any loan; (6) be a U. S. citizen or eligible noncitizen; (7) sign an Anti-Drug Abuse Act Certification (8) be pursuing an undergraduate degree. Priority is given to Federal Pell Grant recipients. The maximum award per student is $4,000 each year.

(193) Federal Perkins Loans. Federal Student Financial Aid Information Center 1 (800) 433-3243, TDD (line for hearing impaired people) 1 (800) 730-8913. Criteria: (1) Recipients must demonstrate exceptional financial need; (2) be enrolled or accepted for enrollment at an approved institution; (3) be enrolled at least halftime; (4) not owe a refund on any grant; (5) be in default on any loan; (6) be a U. S. citizen or eligible noncitizen; (7) sign an Anti-Drug Abuse Act Certification (8) be pursuing an undergraduate degree and up to $15,000 may be borrowed (no more than $3,000 in any one year). Students without a need do not get accepted.

(194) Federal Stafford Loans. Federal Student Financial Aid Information Center 1 (800) 433-3243, TDD (line for hearing impaired people) 1 (800) 730-8913. Criteria: (1) be enrolled or accepted for enrollment at an approved institution (2) be enrolled at least halftime (3) not owe a refund on any grant (4) be in default on any loan (5) be a U. S. citizen or eligible noncitizen (6) sign an Anti-Drug Abuse Act Certification (8) be pursuing an undergraduate degree and up to $15,000 may be borrowed (no more than $3,000 in any one year). Students without a need do not get unsubsidized loans. For graduate or professional study, the maximum award per student is $2,300. Deadline: Apply as soon as possible after January 2. No application will be accepted after May 1.

There are no exceptions to this deadline. Request a free booklet implemented in January, 1998. For more details, contact the financial aid office at the institution of higher education you plan to attend. Loans are a maximum of $30,000 - including any outstanding Perkins Loans borrowed as an undergraduate (no more than $5,000 in any one year). These loans are low-interest.

Part of your loan may be cancelled for you Contact the above for details on this loan program possibly will experience federal budget cuts within the next several years.

A free booklet listing all of the additional details about Federal Government sponsored programs is available from the Federal Student Aid Information Center, P. O. Box 84, Washington, DC 20044.

(195) Federal Direct Student Loans. Federal Student Financial Aid Information Center 1 (800) 433-3243, TDD (line for hearing impaired people) 1 (800) 730-8913. This new program consists of Federal Direct Stafford Loans (subsidized and unsubsidized) and Federal Direct PLUS loans (for parents of dependent college students).

It is essentially the same type of program as the Federal Stafford Loans described above. The difference is that the U. S. Department of Education is the lender rather than a bank or credit union.

Inquire about the Direct Consolidation Loans and Federal PLUS Loans used by parents' of students at (800) 848-0982.

A free booklet listing all of the additional details about Federal Government sponsored loan programs is available from Federal Student Aid Information Center, P. O. Box 84, Washington, DC 20044.

(196) Federal Work Study. Federal Student Financial Aid Information Center 1 (800) 433-3243, TDD (line for hearing impaired people) 1 (800) 730-8913. Criteria: This campus-based program is administered by the financial aid administrator at each participating school.

Money is given directly to the schools to provide jobs for undergraduate and graduate students who need financial aid; when that money is gone, there are no more funds for jobs that year.

The program is open to both undergraduate and graduate students who can demonstrate financial need. Salaries are at least minimum wage ($5.45 per hour); many are higher. Undergraduates are paid by the hour. Undergraduates are either paid by the hour or receive a salary. Total salaries cannot exceed the amount established as students' Federal Work Study Award. A free booklet listing all of the additional details about Federal Government sponsored programs is available from Federal Student Aid Information Center, P. O. Box 84, Washington, DC 20044.

(197) Fellowships. Washington, DC 25060 (202) 287-3271, Internet: SIOFG@SIVM.SI.EDU Request application materials by mail and allow at least 2 weeks for service in the continental U. S. to be made. Appointments carry at least a $250 weekly stipend.

(198) Fellowships. Rollan D. Melton Fellowship is for college-level journalism educators who are members of an ethnic group or who are exceptionally active in teaching journalism to ethnic group members, to attend an American Press Institute seminar of his or her choice.

The fellowship provides tuition, room and meals. For details, write: American Press Institute, 11690 Sunrise Valley Drive, Reston, VA 22091.

(199) Fellowships-Architecture. The American Institute of Architects/The American Architectural Foundation Scholarship Programs, The American Institute of Architects, 1735 New York Avenue, N .W., Washington, DC 20006-5292.

These are cosponsored with the American Hospital Association and are available for graduate students in health facilities design. The Richard Morris Hunt Fellowship is open to architects interested in historic preserva tion. Deadline: January 15.

(200) Fellowships-Composers. Public Information Office, Room 803, National Endowment for the Arts, Nancy Hanks Center, 1100 Pennsylvania Avenue, N. W., Washington, DC 20506-0001 (202) 682-5400, (202) 682-5496 Voice/TT. (Text-Telephone for people who are hearing impaired). Call or write for application packet and guidelines.

(201) Fellowships-Economics. Director, The Knight-Bagehot Fellowship, Graduate School of Journalism, Columbia University, New York, NY 10027, (212) 854-2711 or 854-6840 Fax: (212) 854-7837. You must have at least 4 years experience to apply. Tuition is $17,637 each for 8 recipients and each receive a $16,000 stipend.

(202) Fellowships-Food. Institute of Food Technologists, 221 North LaSalle Street, Chicago, IL 60601 (312) 782-8424 Fax: (312) 782-8348. For graduate students. Numerous grants are provided by: Coca-Cola Foundation, Lipton Foundation, Nabisco Foods, General Mills, Kraft General Foods Foundation, Institute of Food Technologists Past Presidents, Pfizer Food Science Group--Lite Food Ingredients, Grocery Manufacturers of America, Inc., Procter & Gamble Co., Frito-Lay, Inc. Kalsec, Inc.--In honor of Stephen S. Chang, Society of Flavor Chemists Memorial, IFT New York Section, Florasynth, Inc. & etc.

Request information about the Scholarship Program from the Institute of Food Technologists at the address listed above. Grants awards are from $1,250-$5,000.

(203) Fellowships-Jazz. Public Information Office, Room 803, National Endowment for the Arts, Nancy Hanks Center, 1100 Pennsylvania Avenue, N. W., Washington, DC 20506-0001 (202) 682-5400, (202) 682-5496 Voice/TT. (Text Telephone for people who are hearing impaired). Call or write for application packet and guidelines.

(204) Fellowships-Journalism. Director, The Knight-Bagehot Fellowship, Graduate School of Journalism, Columbia University, New York, NY 10027, (212) 854-2711 or 854-6840 Fax: (212) 854-7837. You must have at least 4 years experience to apply. Tuition is $17,637 each for 8 recipients and each receive a $16,000 stipend.

(205) Fellowships-Playwrights. National Endowment for the Arts, Literature Program/Fellowships, Rm. 729, Nancy-Hanks Center, 1100 Pennsylvania Ave., N. W., Washington, D. C. Write for an application and guidelines.

(206) Fellowships Pre-doctoral, Post-doctoral. American Institute of Pakistan Studies, P. O. Box 7568, Wake Forest University, Winston-Salem, NC 27109, (919)759-5453/5449 Fax: (919) 759-6104.

(207) Fellowships-Social Sciences. Albert Einstein Institution Fellowships, 1430 Massachusetts Ave., Cambridge, MA 02138. (617) 876-0311 Fax: (617)876-0837. Write for an application. Stipends are available for 12-month interims. Deadline: January 1 each year.

(208) Fellowships-Social Sciences. Social Science Research Council, 605 Third Avenue, New York, NY, 10158 (212) 661-0280. Numerous fellowships and grants for training and research at the graduate, dissertation and doctorate levels.

(209) Fellowships-Solo Recitalists. Public Information Office, Room 803, National Endowment for the Arts, Nancy Hanks Center, 1100 Pennsylvania Avenue, N. W., Washington, DC 20506-0001 (202) 682-5400, (202) 682-5496 Voice/ TT. (Text-Telephone for people who are hearing impaired). Call or write for application packet and guidelines.

(210) Fine Arts-Doctorate. Jacob K. Javits Fellowships Program, P. O. Box 419, Iowa City, Iowa 52244, 1-800-4-FED-AID. Eligibility is limited to students who at the time of application have no more than 30-semester hours or 45, or the equivalent of graduate credits.

This program provides one year awards with up to four years of renewal, stipends up to $14,400 or the Fellow's financial need whichever is less; also, there is an annual payment of $9,243 for tuition and fees to the school attended.

(211) Fine Arts-Graduate. Jacob K. Javits Fellowships Program, P. O. Box 419, Iowa City, Iowa 52244, 1-800-4-FED-AID. Eligibility is limited to students who at the time of application have no more than 30-semester hours or 45-quarter hours or the equivalent of graduate credits.

This program provides one year awards with up to four years of renewal, stipends up to $14,400 or the Fellow's financial need whichever is less. Also, there is an annual payment of $9,243 for tuition and fees to the school attended.

(212) Fisheries-Undergraduate. Dr. J. Frances Allen Scholarship, 5410 Grosvenor Lane, Suite 110, Bethesda, MD 20814-2199. Program provides one year awards with up to four years of renewal, stipends up to $14,400 or the Fellow's financial need whichever is less, and an annual payment of $9,243 for tuition and fees to the school attended.

(213) Food-Undergraduate. Institute of Food Technologists, 221 North LaSalle Street, Chicago, IL 60601 (312) 782-8424 Fax: (312) 782-8348.

Numerous grants are provided by: Coca-Cola Foundation, Lipton Foundation, Nabisco Foods, Westreco Nestle, Inc. Heinz, U. S. A., Kraft General Foods Foundation, Gerber Companies Foundation, & etc.

Request information about their Scholarship Program. Grants awards are from $750-$2,000 each.

FOREIGN STUDENTS. You should review the College Explorer Plus, a computerized database of United States institutions, at their educational advising office.

Contact the American Embassy in your country. Direct Exchange programs between the United States and another student's home country.

(214) Freedom Forum-Graduate. The Freedom Forum, Freedom Forum World Center, 1101 Wilson Boulevard, Ar-

Arlington, VA 22209. Or call (703)528-0800. Fax: (703)284-2879. A minimum of 50 scholarships will be awarded and the amount is $4,000 per award.

(215) Freedom Forum-Undergraduate. The Freedom Forum, Freedom Forum World Center, 1101 Wilson Boulevard, Arlington, VA 22209. Or call (703)528-0800. Fax: (703)284-2879. A minimum of 50 scholarships will be awarded $4,000 per award.

(216) General-Graduate. Orville Redenbacher Second Start Scholarship Program, P. O. Box 39101, Chicago IL 60639. Criteria: (1) Applicants must be over 30 years old; (2) enrolled in an accredited institution in the United States or Canada; (3) Pass a 500-word essay; (4) have a financial need; (5) be academically competent. Annual awards of $1,000 each are made to 30 recipients. Deadline: May 1 each year.

(217) General-Undergraduate. College Scholarship Information Bank, College Entrance Examination Board, 888 Seventh Avenue, New York, NY 10106. CA 91203

(218) General-Undergraduate. Nestle' U. S. A., Office of Community Affairs, 800 N. Brand Blvd., Glendale, CA 91203.

(219) General-Undergraduate. Avis Rent-A-Car Scholarship, American Society of Travel Agents, 1101 King Street, Alexandria, VA 22314. (703) 739-2782 Fax: (703) 684-8319. Undergraduates must be enrolled in a 2 or 4 year college program with a 2.5 minimum grade point average. One annual award is made in the sum of $3,000. Deadline: June 1.

(220) General-Undergraduate. Herbert Lehman Education Fund, 99 Hudson Street, New York, NY 10013 (212)219-1900. Criteria: (1) Scholarships are only awarded to students who have never been to college (2) You must conform to the interests of the grantor (3) applicants must be citizens of the United States.

(221) General-Undergraduate. Orville Redenbacher Second Start Scholarship Program, P. O. Box 39101, Chicago

IL 60639. Criteria: (1) Applicants must be over 30 years old; (2) enrolled in an accredited institution in the United States or Canada; (3) Pass a 500-word essay; (4) have a financial need; (5) be academically competent. Annual awards of $1,000 each are made to 30 recipients. Deadline: May 1.

(222) Geophysicists-Graduate. SEG Scholarship Foundation Program. P. O. Box 702740, Tulsa, OK 74170-2740. Criteria:

The applicant must intend to pursue a college course directed toward a career in exploration geophysics; must have an interest in and aptitude for physics, mathematics, and geology.

Also, you must be (a) An applicant in need of financial assistance; however, the competence of the student as indicated by the application is given first consideration.

Results of aptitude tests, college entrance exams, National Merit Scholarship Competition, etc., are not required but should be furnished if taken. (b) Certain scholarships administered by the Foundation may carry additional qualifications imposed by the sponsors. Deadline March 1 each year.

(223) Geophysicists-Undergraduate. SEG Scholarship Foundation Program. P. O. Box 702740, Tulsa, OK 74170-2740.

Criteria: The applicant must intend to pursue a college course directed toward a career in exploration geophysics; must have an interest in and aptitude for physics, mathematics, and geology. Also, you must meet the requirements listed in **(222)** above.

National Merit Scholarship Competition, etc., are not required but should be furnished if taken. Certain scholarships administered by the Foundation may carry additional qualifications imposed by the sponsors. Deadline: March 1 each year.

(224) Graphic Arts-Undergraduate. National Scholarships

for Graphic Arts, 4615 Forbes Avenue, Pittsburgh, PA 15213-3796. Scholarship awards are $1,500-$3,000. Deadline: January 15.

(225) Graphic Arts-Undergraduate. Dan Edwards/Rich Conti/Dan Petz, Admissions Representatives. CAD Institute, 4100 East Broadway, Phoenix, AZ 85040 1(800) 658-5744 or (602) 437-0405 Fax: (602) 437-5695.

Criteria: (1) Applicant cannot be a resident of Arizona; (2) must have a High School diploma (or GED) or about to graduate high school in the current school year.

Approximate scholarship value is $15,000. Deadline: March 1.

(226) Graphic Communications. National Scholarship Trust Fund Of The Graphic Arts, 4615 Forbes Avenue, Pittsburgh, PA 15213-3796 (412)621-6941.

Criteria: The student must be interested in a career in graphic communications and he or she must be a high school senior or a high school graduate who has not yet started college. Scholarship awards vary in amount from $500-1,000 in an academic year.

(227) Health-Allopathic Medicine. Division of Student Assistance. BHPR/HRSA. Student and Institutional Support Branch, Parklawn Blvd., Rm. 8-34, 5600 Fishers Lane, Rockville, MD 20857, (301)443-4776,

This program is made available to accredited public or non-profit schools of medicine. Inquire to find how you can be considered for assistance.

(228) Health-Allopathic Medicine. National Health Service Corps Scholarship Program, 1010 Wayne Avenue, Suite 1200, Silver Spring, MD 20910 1(800) 638-0824.

Criteria: (1) U. S. citizens enrolled or accepted for enrollment in accredited U.S. Schools of Allopathic Medicine.

(229) Health-Dental Hygienists Certificate/Associate Degree. American Dental Hygienists' Association, 444 North Michigan Avenue Suite 3400, Chicago, IL 60611 (312)440-

8900. Criteria: Document financial need of at least $1,500; (2) Be enrolled in an accredited dental hygiene program in the United States 3) Have completed a minimum of one year in a dental hygiene curriculum.

(230) Health-Dental Hygienists Doctorate. American Dental Hygienists' Association, 444 North Michigan Avenue Suite 3400, Chicago, IL 60611 (312)440-8900 .

Criteria: Document financial need of at least $1,500; (2) Be enrolled the year for which you are applying unless applying for the designated Part-time Scholarship (3) Have completed a award; (4) Have a minimum grade point average of 3.0 (on a 4.0 scale) in an accredited dental hygiene program in the United States for the award (5) Be full-time students during the academic year for which you are applying unless applying for the designated Part-time Scholarship. Deadline: April 1.

(231) Health-Dental Hygienists Graduate. American Dental Hygienists' Association, 444 North Michigan Avenue Suite 3400, Chicago, IL 60611 (312) 442-8900.

(232) Health-Dental Hygienists Undergraduate. American Dental Hygienists' Association, 444 North Michigan Avenue Suite 3400, Chicago, IL 60611 (312)440-8900

Criteria: Document financial need of at least $1,500; (2) Be enrolled in an accredited dental hygiene program in the United States; (3) Have completed a minimum of one year in a dental hygiene curriculum prior to receiving an award; (4) Have a minimum grade point average of 3.0 (on a 4.0 scale) for the time you have been enrolled in a dental hygiene curriculum; (5) Be full-time students during the academic year for which you are applying unless applying for the designated Part-time Scholarship. Annual deadline is: April 1.

(233) Health-Dentistry. Division of Student Assistance. BPHR/HRSA. Student and Institutional Support Branch, Parklawn Blvd., Rm. 8-34, 5600 Fishers Lane, Rockville, MD,

20857, (301) 443-4776, This program is made available to accredited public or non-profit schools of medicine. Inquire to find how you can be considered for assistance.

(234) Health-Education Fund. c/o First Florida Bank, N. A., P. O. Box 11311, St. Petersburg, FL 33713. Ten grants of $500 each are awarded. Deadline: Varies.

(235) Health-Hearing Audiology. AMBUCS Scholarships for Therapists, The Living Endowment Fund, Inc., P. O. Box 5127, High Point, NC 27262. Criteria: You must be accepted for enrollment before your application will be reviewed.

(236) Health-Medical Pre-doctoral. National Research Council, Office of Scientific and Engineering Personnel, 2101 Constitution Avenue, Washington, DC 20418, (202) 334-2872, Ford Foundation pre-doctoral and dissertation fellowships are due November 4, of each year.

(237) Health-Medical Studies. Alpha Epsilon Iota, Society Bank Michigan, P. O. Box 8612, Ann Arbor, MI 48107-8612. (313)994-5555. For students who are entering their first year of medical school.

(238) Health-Medical Studies. Fulbright-Hays Institute of International Education, Department of Education, Office of Education, Washington, DC 20202. Students pursuing medical degrees should write for information.

(239) Health-Medicine. Professions Scholarship Program For Medicine, Department of The Army U. S. Army Health Professional Support Agency, The Curtis Center, Suite 460 West, Independence Square West, 601 Walnut Street, Philadelphia, PA 19106-3399. (215) 597-6871 or 6872.

(240) Health-Medicine. Council for International Exchange of Scholars (CIES), 3400 International Dr., N. W., Washington, DC 20008, (202) 686-4000. Department of Education, Office of Education, Washington, DC 20202.

(241) Health-Music Therapy. AMBUCS Scholarships for Therapists, The Living Endowment Fund, Inc., P. O. Box 5127, High Point, NC 27262. Criteria: You must be accepted for enrollment before your application will be reviewed.

(242) Health-Nurse Midwifery Graduate. National Health Service Corps Scholarship Program, 1010 Wayne Avenue, Suite 1200, Silver Spring, MD 20910 1(800) 638-0824. Criteria: (1) U. S. citizens enrolled or accepted for enrollment in accredited U. S. Schools of Nursing Medicine.

(243) Health-Nurse Practitioner Graduate. National Health Service Corps Scholarship Program, 1010 Wayne Avenue, Suite 1200, Silver Spring, MD 20910 1 (800) 638-0824. Criteria: (1) U. S. citizens enrolled or accepted for enrollment in accredited U. S. Schools of Nursing.

(244) Health-Nursing. Navy Nurse Corps NROTC Scholarship Program. Navy-Marine Corps ROTC, College Scholarships Program, CDR Navy Recruiting Command Code 314, 801 North Randolph Street, Arlington, VA 22203-9705. 1-800-NAV-ROTC. Four-year NROTC scholarships are available to students interested in pursuing bachelor of science degrees in nursing (BSN).

If selected for a scholarship, the selectee must major in a nursing degree program leading to a BSN. NROTC Scholarship Program requirements include academic, physical and military standards. Write or call and request more information.

(245) Health-Nursing. Epilepsy Foundation of America, Behavioral Sciences Fellowships, Research Administration, 4351 Garden City Drive, Landover, MD 20785. (301) 459-3700. Criteria: Research that relates to epilepsy must be conducted. Deadline: March 1 each year.

(246) Health-Occupational Therapy. American Occupational Therapy Foundation, 4720 Montgomery Lane, P. O. Box 31220, Bethesda, MD 20824-1220. Send $1 with your request for an application.

(247) Health-Occupational Therapy. AMBUCS Scholarships for Therapists, The Living Endowment Fund, Inc., P.

O. Box 5127, High Point, NC 27262. Criteria: You must be accepted for enrollment before your application will be reviewed.

(248) Health-Occupational Therapy-Graduate. American Occupational Therapy Foundation, 4720 Montgomery Lane P. O. Box 31220, Bethesda, MD 20824-1220. Send $1 with your request for an application.

(249) Health-Occupational Therapy Undergraduate. American Occupational Therapy Foundation, 4720 Montgomery Lane, P. O. Box 31220, Bethesda, MD 20824-1220. Send $1 with your request for an application.

(250) Health-Oral. American Dental Hygienists' Association. Proctor & Gamble Oral Health/ ADHA Institute Scholarship Program, 444 N. Michigan Avenue, Suite 3400, Chicago, IL 60611.

(251) Health-Osteopathic Medicine. Division of Student Assistance. BHPR/HRSA. Student and Institutional Support Branch, Parklawn Blvd., Rm. 8-34, 5600 Fishers Lane, Rockville, MD 20857, (301) 443-4776, This program is made available to accredited public or non-profit schools of medicine. Inquire to find how you can be considered for assistance.

(252) Health-Osteopathic Medicine. National Health Service Program requirements include academic, physical and military standards. Write or call and request more information.

Twenty-five $1,000 Scholarships are available. Corps Scholarship Program, 1010 Wayne Avenue, Suite 1200, Silver Spring, MD 20910 1 (800) 638-0824. Criteria: (1) U. S. citizens enrolled for accepted for enrollment in accredited U. S. Schools of Osteopathic Medicine.

(253) Health-Physical Education. NSCA Challenge Scholarships, National Strength and Conditioning Association, P. O. Box 81410, Lincoln, NE 68501, Contact Lore Warner, Grants awards are $1,000. Deadline: April 16 each year.

(254) Health-Physical Therapy. AMBUCS Scholarships for Therapists, The Living Endowment Fund, Inc., P. O. Box 5127, High Point, NC 27262. Criteria: You must be accepted for enrollment before your application will be reviewed.

(255) Health-Physical Therapy. NSCA Challenge Scholarships, National Strength and Conditioning Association, P. O. Box 81410, Lincoln, NE 68501,

Contact Lore Warner, Grants awards are $1,000. Deadline: April 16 each year.

(256) Health-Physical Therapy. Doctoral Foundation for Physical Therapy, Trans-Potomac Plaza No. 3, 1055 N. Fairfax Street., Suite 350, Alexandria, VA 22314, (703)684-5984, Fax: (703)684-3218. Maximum awards for $12,000 can be requested. Deadline: February 15.

(257) Health-Physical Therapy. AMBUCS Scholarships for Therapists, The Living Endowment Fund, Inc., P. O. Box 5127, High Point, NC 27262.

Criteria: You must be accepted for enrollment before your application will be reviewed.

(258) Health-Physician Assistant-Graduate. National Health Service Corps Scholarship Program, 1010 Wayne Avenue, Suite 1200, Silver Spring, MD 20910 1 (800) 638-0824.

Criteria: (1) U. S. citizens enrolled or accepted for enrollment in accredited U. S. Schools of Medicine.

(259) Health-Physician Assistant-Undergraduate. National Health Service Corps Scholarship Program, 1010 Wayne Avenue, Suite 1200, Silver Spring, MD 20910 1 (800) 638-0824. Criteria: (1) U. S. citizens enrolled for accepted for enrollment in accredited U. S. Schools of Medicine.

(260) Health-Speech Pathology. NSCA Challenge Scholarships, National Strength and Conditioning Association, P. O. Box 81410, Lincoln, NE 68501, Contact Lore Warner, Grants awards are $1,000. Deadline: April 16, each year.

(261) Health-Therapeutic Recreation. AMBUCS Scholarships for Therapists, The Living Endowment Fund, Inc., P. O. Box 5127, High Point, NC 27262. Criteria: You must be accepted for enrollment before your application will be reviewed.

(262) High School Students-Art. The Scholastic Art Awards, Attn: Unsponsored Fee, 555 Broadway, New York, NY 10012. Have a teacher submit not more than 10 portfolios and send an application fee of $60.00.

More than $350,000 in awards and scholarships are made. This is the largest program of its kind in the nation. You get a chance to show your work in the Scholastic Art Awards National Exhibition. Write for guidelines.

(263) High School Students-Geophysicists. Those interested in becoming Geophysicists. SEG Scholarship Foundation Program. P. O. Box 702740, Tulsa, OK 74170-2740. Criteria: The applicant must intend to pursue a college course directed toward a career in exploration geophysics; must have an interest in and aptitude for physics, mathematics, and geology.

Also, you must be (a) A high school student with above average grades planning to enter college the next fall term (b) An applicant in need of financial assistance will be considered; however, the competence of the student as indicated by the application is given first consideration. Results of aptitude tests, college entrance exams, will be assessed.

National Merit Scholarship Competition, etc., are not required but should be furnished if taken. (c) Certain scholarships administered by the Foundation may carry additional qualifications imposed by the sponsors. Deadline: March 1 of each year.

(264) High School Students-Golf. Evans Golf Caddie Scholarship, Evans Scholars Foundation c/o Western Golf Association, Golf, IL 60029, (708) 724-4600. Criteria: Start your application process during your junior year in high school.

Request an application as soon as possible after July 1. Additional requirements should be obtained from the committee-call or write.

(265) High School Students-Graphic Arts. National Scholarships for Graphic Arts, 4615 Forbes Avenue, Pittsburgh, PA 15213-3796. Scholarship awards are $1,500-$3,000. Deadline: January 15.

(266) High School Students-Science. Westinghouse Science Talent Search, Science Service, Inc., 1719 N Street N. W., Washington, DC 20036 (202) 785-2255. Forty finalists are chosen from among 300 semifinalists who are selected from some 1,600 entrants.

The forty receive an all-expenses-paid trip to Washington to compete for Westinghouse Science Scholarships totaling $205,000. The first place scholarship is $40,000.

(267) High School Students-Writers. The Scholastic Writing Awards. The Scholastic Art Awards, 555 Broadway, New York, NY 10012. All students in grades 7-12 who are currently enrolled in public or non-public schools in the United States of America.

(268) Honors Society. Phi Beta Kappa Society, Mary Isabel Sibley Fellowship, 1811 Q Street, N. W., Washington, DC 20009. (202) 265-3808. Applicants must file before January 15 of the year in which the award is granted; recipients will be notified before April 1.

(269) Humanities-Doctorate. Jacob K. Javits Fellowships Program, P. O. Box 419, Iowa City, Iowa 52244, 1-800-4-FED-AID. Eligibility is limited to students who at the time of application have no more than 30-semester hours or 45-quarter hours or equivalent of graduate credits.

This Program provides one year awards with up to four years of renewal, stipends up to $14,400 or the Fellow's financial need whichever is less, and an annual payment of $9,243 for tuition and fees to the school attended.

(270) Humanities-Graduate. Jacob K. Javits Fellowships Program, P. O. Box 419, Iowa City, Iowa 52244, 1-800-4-FED-AID. Eligibility is limited to students who at the time of application have no more than 30-semester hours or 45-quarter hours or equivalent of graduate credits.

This Program provides one year awards with up to four years of renewal, stipends up to $14,400 or the Fellow's financial need whichever is less, and an annual payment of $9,243 for tuition and fees to the school attended.

(271) Industrial Education. National Scholarships Trust Fund, 4615 Forbes Avenue, Pittsburgh, PA 15213. (412) 621-6941 Fax: (412) 621-3049. You must be pursuing an education as it has an application to the printing, publishing and packaging industries.

(272) International Studies-Graduate. Deputy Director, Human Rights Watch, 485 Fifth Avenue, New York, NY 10017. Those selected for the Orville Sevill Fellowship in international human rights will work full- time for one year for one or more components of the Human Rights Watch.

Criteria: Exceptional analytic skills, an ability to work and speak clear and a commitment to work in the human rights field on a paid or volunteer basis. The salary is $25,000 plus benefits. Deadline: January 1.

A Message About Internships.

Some concerns you should share with your Internship sponsor are the following: Many companies require that you drive a car. Inquire to find whether you will be expected to bring one to your internship site.

Will you be required to have some skills in the area you are seeking your internship studies? Most often computer literacy is a minimum ability. Some require interviews before your acceptance.

Are you willing to travel to another state at your own expense? Is your Internship salary at least the minimum you will accept? What do you expect to gain from your

Internship? Are you prepared to send in samples of your completed work in your internship field?

(273) Internships-Broadcast. Dow Jones Newspaper Fund, P. O. Box 300, Princeton, NJ 08543-0300. (609)452-2820. Forty-five internships are annually awarded, $1,000 scholarships. Applications are available from October 1 - November 1. Deadline: November 15.

(274) Internships-Business. Newsletter of Organizations Offering Internships. Bernard Ford, President, Ford & Ford-Careerworks, 105 Chestnut, Suite 34, Needham, MA 01292

(275) Internships-Journalism. Dow Jones Newspaper Fund, P. O. Box 300, Princeton, NJ 08543-0300. (609)452-2820. Forty-five internships are annually awarded, $1,000 scholarships. Applications are available from October 1-November 1. Deadline: November 15.

(276) Internships-Radio, Television & Film. Dow Jones Newspaper Fund, P. O. Box 300, Princeton, NJ 08543-0300. (609) 452-2820. Forty-five internships are annually awarded, $1,000 scholarships. Applications are available from October 1-November 1. Deadline: November 15.

(277) Internships-Science. Science Service, Inc., 1719 N. Street, N. W., Washington, DC 20036 (202) 785-2255. "Science News" enhances the public understanding of science. Each year, two or three specially qualified students work as members of the staff.

The rigorous training and invaluable experience they get during this internship is excellent preparation for their careers in science journalism.

(278) Internships. The Wesleyan Challenge. P. O. Box 7070, Wesleyan University, Middletown, CT 06459. 1 (800) 43-WES-GO.

Students have an opportunity to receive $2,000-$5,000 for implementation of a summer service project that will improve their community plus a $3,000 scholarship to a college of their choice. Write the above address.

(279) Internships-Zoology. National Zoological Traineeships, National Zoological Park, Washington, D C   20008. (202) 673-4950 Fax (202) 673-4738.

(280) Journalism. National Newspaper Foundation Serrill Scholarships, National Newspaper Association, 1525 Wilson Boulevard, Suite 550, Arlington, VA 22209-2434 1(800) 829-4661 (703) 907-7900 Fax: (703) 907-7901.

(281) Journalism. William B. Ruggles Scholarship. The Selection Committee, c/o National Right to Work Committee, 8001 Braddock Road, Suite 500, Springfield, VA 22100.

Applicants must demonstrate potential for successful completion of educational requirements in an accredited journalism program.

Recipient must demonstrate an understanding of volunteerism and of the problems of compulsory unionism. A $2,000 scholarship is available to the student who exemplifies the dedication of Mr. Ruggles. Applications must be submitted between January 1, and March 31, of each calendar year.

(282) Journalism-Broadcast. Dow Jones Newspaper Fund, P. O. Box 300, Princeton, NJ 08543-0300 (609) 452-2820. Scholarships are given to full-time undergraduate students pursuing a career in print journalism at a four-year college or university.

Scholarships will be distributed as follows: Up to 20 each freshmen and sophomores selected get $1,000. Thirty-seven juniors and forty seniors selected will each receive $3,000.

(283) Journalism-Electronic. Radio and Television News Directors Foundation. RTNDF Scholarships, 1000 Connecticut Avenue, NW, Suite 615, Washington, DC 20036.

The Len Allen Award of Merit, a $1,000 scholarship is available to students of electronic journalism who display both expertise and interest in pursuing further training in the areas of electronic journalism. Deadline: March 1.

(284) Journalism-Graduate. Deputy Director, Human Rights Watch, 485 Fifth Avenue, New York, NY 10017. Those selected for the Orville Sevill Fellowship in International Human Rights will work full-time for one year for one or more components of the Human Rights Watch. Criteria: (1) Exceptional analytic skills; (2) an ability to work; (3) speak clear; (4) a commitment to work in the human rights field on a paid or volunteer basis. The salary is $25,000 plus benefits. Deadline: January 1.

(285) Journalism-Graduate. Dow Jones Newspaper Fund, P. O. Box 300, Princeton, NJ 08543-0300. (609) 452-2820. Forty-five internships are annually awarded, $1,000 scholarships. Applications are available from October 1-November1. Deadline: November 15.

(286) Journalism-Print. Dow Jones Newspaper Fund, P. O. Box 300, Princeton, NJ 08543-0300 (609) 452-2820. Scholarships are given to full-time undergraduate students pursuing a career in print journalism at a four-year college or university.

Scholarships will be distributed as follows: Up to 20 each freshmen and sophomores selected get $1,000. Thirty-seven juniors and forty seniors selected will each receive $3,000.

(287) Journalism-Undergraduate. Dow Jones Newspaper Fund, P. O. Box 300, Princeton, NJ 08543-0300. (609) 452-2820. Forty-five internships are annually awarded, $1,000 scholarships. Applications are available from October 1-November 1. Deadline: November 15. U. S. Territories, U. S.- sponsored schools abroad and Canada are eligible.

There are 4 scholarships of $5,000 each for the best portfolios submitted by this year's graduating students. Total pages are not to exceed 50 pages. Portfolio awards also are available for sponsoring teachers. Entry deadline is January 14 of each year.

(288) Journalism-Undergraduate. Helen Miller Malloch

Scholarship, National Federation of Press Women, Inc., P. O. Box 99, Blue Springs, MO 64013. (816) 229-1666. $500-$1,000 grants awarded. Deadline: May 1

(289) Journalism-Undergraduate. Robert P. Scripps Graphic Arts Grants, Scripps Howard Foundation, P. O. Box 5380, Cincinnati, OH 45201. (513)977-3036 Fax: (513) 977-3810. You must annually apply for the maximum scholarship in the amount of $3,000. Deadline: February 25.

(290) Law-Deputy Director, Human Rights Watch, 485 Fifth Avenue, New York, NY 10017. Those selected for the Orville Sevill Fellowship in international human rights will work full-time for one year for one or more components of the Human Rights Watch.

Criteria: (1) Exceptional analytic skills; (2) an ability to work; (3) speak clear; (4) a commitment to work in the human rights field on a paid or volunteer basis. The salary is $25,000 plus benefits. Deadline: January 1.

(291) Law. Herbert Lehman Education Fund, 99 Hudson Street, New York, NY 10013 (212)219-1900. Criteria: (1) Scholarships are only awarded to students who have never been to college (2) You must conform to the interests of the grantor (3) Applicants must be citizens of the United States.

(292) Law. Assistance for training in the legal profession. Council on Legal Education Opportunity (CLEO) 1800 M. Street, N. W., Suite 160 South Lobby, Washington, DC 20036, (202) 785-4840. assistance with placement in a law school.

Stipends during attendance at law school for up to three years. Closing Date: January 1, of the year you want to apply to a college or university.

(293) Liberal Arts-Undergraduate. Arthur C. & Lucia S. Palmer Foundation Grants, H. Slade Palmer, President, 471 Pennsylvania Avenue., Waverly, NY 14892. (607)565-4603. Grants awards are $250-$1000 per semester. Deadline: April 30 each year.

(294) Library And Information Studies-Graduate. Ameri-

COLLEGE: HOW TO GET THERE AND GO FREE

can Library Association, Office for Library Personnel Resources and the Standing Committee on Library Education 50 E. Huron Street, Chicago, IL 60611-2795.

Financial aid is in the form of scholarships, teaching and research assistantships, grants, work-study, loans and tuition assistance.

(295) Literature-Graduate. National Endowment for the Arts cooperative graduate placement and dual degree programs. Approximately $250,000 is available for scholarships.

(296) Loans-Educational. Office of Financial Aid, Presbyterian Church (USA) 100 Witherspoon Street, Louisville, KY 40202 1396. Criteria: (1) Applicants must be members of the Presbyterian Church (U.S.A.); (2) Be U. S. Citizens or permanent residents of the U. S.; (3) Be in good academic standing; (4) Demonstrate financial need; (5) Give satisfactory evidence of financial reliability; (6) Be enrolled full-time; (6) Be working toward a degree in a college or university that is fully accredited by its regional accrediting association. These loans are for graduate and undergraduate students. The range of loans is $200-$1,000.

(297) Loans-Educational. Federal Perkins Loans, Federal Student Financial Aid Information Center 1 (800) 433-3243, TDD (line for hearing impaired people) 1 (800) 730-8913. Criteria: (1) Recipients must demonstrate exceptional financial need; (2) be enrolled or accepted for enrollment at an approved institution; (3) be enrolled at least halftime; (4) not owe a refund on any grant; (5) be in default on any loan; (6) be a U. S. citizen or eligible noncitizen; (7) sign an Anti-Drug Abuse Act Certification (8) be pursuing an undergraduate degree and up to $15,000 may be borrowed (no more than $3,000 in any one year). For graduate or professional study, up to a maximum of $30,000 - including any outstanding Perkins Loans borrowed as an undergraduate (no more than $5,000 in any one year).

The loans are low-interest. Part of your loan may be cancelled for you. This program may possibly be experiencing federal budget cuts within the next several years.

A free booklet listing all of the additional details about Federal Government sponsored programs is available from Federal Student Aid Information Center, P. O. Box 84, Washington, DC 20044.

(298) Loans - Educational Nursing. Nursing Education Loan Repayment. U. S. Department of Health and Human Services, Public Health Resources and Service Administration Public Health Service Health Resources and Service Administration, Bureau of Primary Health Care, The Division of Scholarships and Loan Repayments, Twinbrook Metro Plaza Building, Room 620, 12300 Twinbrook Pkwy, Rockville, MD. (301)443-0743 Fax: (301)443-9350.

(299) Mathematics-Graduate. Electrical Cooperative Developmental Energy Program.Forat Valley State College, Fort Valley, GA.

The program provides summer internships, cooperative graduate placement and dual degree programs. Approximately $250,000 is available for scholarships.

(300) Mathematics-Graduate Geoscience. Cooperative Developmental Energy Program, Forat Valley State College, Fort Valley, GA.

The program provides summer internships, cooperative graduate placement and dual degree programs. Approximately $250,000 is available for scholarships

(301) Mathematics-Undergraduate. National Scholarships Trust Fund, 4615 Forbes Avenue, Pittsburgh, PA 15213. (412)621-6941 Fax: (412)621-3049. You must be pursuing an education as it has an application to the printing, publishing and packaging industries.

(302) Mortuary Science-Undergraduate. American Board of Funer l Service Education, 14 Crestwood Road., Cumberland, ME 04021. Twenty-five to fifty grants of either

ther $250 or $500 will be awarded.

(303) Older Adult Service Information System. (OASIS) Directory of Learning Opportunities for Older Persons, American Association of Retired Persons Fulfillment, 601 E Street, N. W., Washington, DC 20049. Lists data about summer, weekend and other learning programs. Request Publication D13973.

(304) People With Disabilities -Blind. Opportunities for the Blind, Inc., P. O. Box 510, Leonardtown, MD 20650 (301)862-1990. Grants awards are between $1,000-$5,000. Deadlines are: Feb 15, May 15, August 15, and November 15 each year.

(305) People With Disabilities-Blind. American Foundation for the Blind, Inc., 15 West 16th Street, New York, NY 10011 (212)620-2043 Fax:(212)675-5037. Grants awards are $1,000.

(306) People With Disabilities-Blind Undergraduate. Floyd Qualls Scholarship For the Blind, Post-Secondary Students, American Council of the Blind, 1155-15th Street, N. W., Suite 720, Washington, DC 20005. (202)467-5081. $1,000-$2,000 grants are annually awarded. Deadline: March 15 each year.

(307) People With Disabilities-Blind Undergraduate. National Federation of the Blind Scholarship Committee. Grinnell State Bank Bldg., 2nd Fl., 814 Fourth Avenue, Grinnell, Iowa 50112. (515)236-3366. The persons who are legally blind and studying in a post-secondary institution will when accepted, receive scholarships valued at no less than $2,000 and the top scholarship that is for $10,000. The Deadline: March 31 each year.

(308) People With Disabilities-Blind Vocational/Technical. Floyd Qualls Scholarship For the Blind, Post-Secondary Students, American Council of the Blind, 1155-15th Street, N. W., Suite 720, Washington, DC 20005. (202) 467-5081. $1,000-$2,000 grants are annually awarded. Deadline:

March 15 each year.

(309) People With Disabilities-Deaf. National Fraternal Society of the Deaf Scholarships, 1300 W. Northwest Hwy., Mount Prospect, IL 60056. (708) 392-9282, Fax-(708) 392-9298. Ten annual awards $750 each are given. Deadline: July 1 each year..

(310) Physics-Undergraduate. National Scholarships Trust Fund, 4615 Forbes Avenue, Pittsburgh, PA 15213. (412) 621-6941 Fax: (412) 621-3049. You must be pursuing an education as it has an application to the printing, publishing and packaging industries.

(311) Political Science-Undergraduate. Epilepsy Foundation of America, Behavioral Sciences Fellowships, Research Administration, 4351 Garden City Drive, Landover, MD 20785. (301) 459-3700.

Criteria: Research that relates to epilepsy must be conducted. Deadline: March 1 each year.

(312) Psychology, Epilepsy Foundation of America, Behavioral Sciences Fellowships, Research Administration, 4351 Garden City Drive, Landover, MD 20785. (301) 459-3700.

Criteria: Research that relates to epilepsy must be conducted. Deadline: March 1 each year.

(313) Public Servants-Graduate. The Harry S. Truman Scholarship Foundation, 712 Jackson Place, N.W., Washington, DC 20006, (202)395-4831, Fax: (202) 395-6995.

Criteria: For Juniors at a four-year institution or a sophomore at a two-year institution. You must be enrolled in an accredited institution of higher education and a committed student.

(314) Public Servants-Undergraduate. The Harry S. Truman Scholarship Foundation, 712 Jackson Place, N.W., Washington, DC 20006, (202)395-4831, Fax: (202) 395-6995.

Criteria: For juniors at a four-year institution or a sophomore at a two-year institution. You must be en rolled in an accredited institution of higher education, committed to a career in public service, United States citizen or a United States of America national. Awards are for up to $6,000 per year for 2 years.Deadline: December 2, each year.

(315) Radio, Television & Film-Graduate. Dow Jones Newspaper Fund, P. O. Box 300, Princeton, NJ 08543-0300. (609)452-2820. Forty-five internships are annually awarded $1,000 scholarships. Applications are available from October 1-November 1. Deadline: November 15.

(316) Radio, Television & Film-Undergraduate. Dow Jones Newspaper Fund, P. O. Box 300, Princeton, NJ 08543-0300. (609)452-2820. Forty-five internships are annually awarded, $1,000 scholarships. Applications are available from October 1-November 1. Deadline: November 15.

(317) Religion-Catholic. Knights of Columbus, Supreme Office, Columbus Plaza, New Haven, Connecticut 06510, (203)772-2130. Criteria: The applicant's father must be a member in good standing of the Knights of Columbus or if deceased, the father must have been a member in good standing at the time of his death.

You must be a high school senior and planning to enter a four year college next September. You must attend a Catholic college or university in the United States. Deadline: March 1.

(318) Religion-Christian. Christian Women's Scholarships. Women of the ELCA Scholarship Program, 8765 West Higgins Road, Chicago, IL 60631-419.

Criteria: You must be 21 years of age or older and you must have experienced an interruption in your schooling at least 2 years since high school. You must be a laywoman. Deadline: March 1.

(319) Religion-Episcopal. Episcopal Theology Evangelical Education Society, 2300 9th Street S. Suite 301, Arlington, VA 22204-2351. (703) 521-3264. Grants awards are $500-1,000 each year.

116

(320) Religion-Jewish-Christian. Teachers can apply for Christian studies through the Sister Rose Thering, Endowment for Jewish-Christian Studies. Seton Hall University, South Orange, NJ 07079 (202) 761-9770 or Fax: (202) 761-9596.

(321) Religion-Lutheran. Aid Association For Lutherans, 4321 North Ballard Road, Appleton, WI 54919-0001 (414) 734-5721 extension 3010.

Each year, 2,500 scholarships are provided and valued at over $2 million. For information about various programs, call or write.

(322) Religion-Ministry-Males. The Lois and Samuel Silberman Fund, Inc. 133 East 79th Street, New York, NY 10021. (212)737-8500. Deadline: Varies.

(323) Religion Ministry-Males. Heath Educational Fund. c/o First Florida Bank, N. A., P. O. Box 11311, St. Petersburg, FL 33713. Grantor gives 10 grants of $500 each. Deadline: Varies.

(324) Religion-Presbyterian. Office of Financial Aid, Presbyterian Church (USA) 100 Witherspoon Street, Louisville, KY 40202-1396.

Criteria: (1) Applicants must be Citizens or permanent residents of the U. S. (2) Be in good academic standing. (3) Be recommended by the financial aid officer at their theological institution members of the Presbyterian Church (U.S.A.)

(325) Religion-Theology Doctorate-Episcopal. Episcopal Church Foundation Graduate Fellowships, 815 2nd. Avenue, Suite 400, New York, NY 10017. Nomination is by your Dean. Write for information.

Maximum $17,500 awarded to 4-6 recipients each year. Deadline: November 1.

(326) Second-Time College Students. National Association of Returning Students, P. O. Box 3283, Salem, OR 97302 (503) 581-3731.

117

(327) Social Science. Jacob K. Javits Fellowships Program, P. O. Box 419, Iowa City, IA 52244, 1-800-4-FED-AID. Eligibility is limited to students who at the time of application have no more than 30-semester hours or 45-quarter hours or equivalent of graduate credits. This Program provides one year awards with up to four years of renewal, stipends up to $14,400 or the Fellow's financial need whichever is less, and an annual payment of $9,243 for tuition and fees to the school attended.

(328) Social Science. Harry Frank Guggenheim Foundation, 90 Park Avenue, New York, NY 10016. (212)687-4470.

You must be at your dissertation level. Deadline: October 1 each year.

(329) Social Science-Doctorate. Albert Einstein Institution Fellowships, 1430 Massachusetts Ave., Cambridge, MA 02138. (617)876-0311 Fax: (617)876-0837. Stipends are available for 12-month interims. Deadline: January 1 each year.

(330) Social Science-Doctorate. Jacob K. Javits Fellowships Program, P. O. Box 419, Iowa City, Iowa 52244, 1-800-4-FED-AID. Eligibility is limited to students who at the time of application have no more than 30-semester hours or 45-quarter hours or equivalent of graduate credits.

This program provides one year awards with up to four years of renewal, stipends up to $14,400 or the Fellow's financial need whichever is less, and an annual grant of $9,243 for tuition and fees to the school attended.

(331) Social Science-Post-Doctorate. Albert Einstein Institution Fellowships, 1430 Massachusetts Ave, Cambridge, MA 02138 (617) 876-0311 . Deadline: January 1 each year.

(332) Social Work. Epilepsy Foundation of America, Behavioral Sciences Fellowships, Research Administration, 4351 Garden City Drive, Landover, MD 20785. (301) 459-3700. Criteria: Research that relates to epilepsy must be conducted. Deadline: March 1 each year.

(333) Social Work. The Lois and Samuel Silberman Fund,

Inc., 133 East 79th Street, New York, NY 10021, (212) 737-8500. Deadline: Varies.

(334) Social Work. Mildred Carter Bradham Fellowship, Zeta Phi Beta Sorority, 1734 New Hampshire Ave., N W., Washington, DC 20009. Grants are in the sums of $500-$1,000 for one academic year.

Criterion: You must be a member. Deadline: February 1 each year.

(335) Social Work-Undergraduate. Epilepsy Foundation of America, Behavioral Sciences Fellowships, Research Administration, 4351 Garden City Drive, Landover, MD 20785. (301) 459-3700.

Criteria: Research that relates to epilepsy must be conducted. Deadline: March 1 each year.

(336) Sociology. Epilepsy Foundation of America, Behavioral Sciences Fellowships, Research Administration, 4351 Garden City Drive, Landover, MD 20785. (301) 459-3700.

Criteria: Research that relates to epilepsy must be conducted. Deadline: March 1 each year.

(337) Sociology-Undergraduate. Epilepsy Foundation of America, Behavioral Sciences Fellowships, Research Administration, 4351 Garden City Drive, Landover, MD 20785. (301) 459-3700.

Criteria: Research that relates to epilepsy must be conducted. Deadline: March 1 each year.

(338) Study/Travel Abroad. American Field Service Intercultural Programs USA, Third Floor, 220 East 42nd Street, New York, NY 10017.

AFS is an international, voluntary nongovernmental, non-profit organization that provides intercultural learning opportunities to help people develop the knowledge, skills, and understanding needed to create a more just and peaceful world.

AFS Programs are available in more than 45 countries. Offers scholarships, local and national financial aid. Request their free "Programs abroad catalog."

(339) Study/Travel Abroad. Council on International Education Exchange, 205 East 42nd. Street, New York, NY 10017-5706.

Administers 38 study abroad programs in 22 countries. Contact them for valuable financial aid resources and excellent travel tips.

Department of Education (Room 3062) 7th & D Streets, S. W., Washington, DC 20202-5331 (202) 708-9291. Deadline: October 30.

(340) Study/Travel Abroad. Fulbright-Hays Doctoral Dissertation Research Abroad. CFDA #84.022A Karla V. B. Block, Center for International Education, U. S. Department of Education (Room 3062) 7th & D Streets, S. W., Washington, DC 20202-5331 (202) 708-9291. Deadline: October 30.

(341) Study/Travel Abroad. Fulbright-Hays Faculty Research Abroad. CFDA #84.019A

Contact: Robert R. Dennis or Michelle LeSound, Center for International Education, U. S. Department of Education (Room 3062) 7th & D Streets, S. W., Washington, DC 20202-5332 (202) 708-7292.

Grant source intentions are to provide grants to scholars to conduct research abroad in modern foreign language and area studies. Deadline: October 30.

(342) Study/Travel Abroad. The Kosciuszko Foundation Domestic Grants Office, 15 East 65th Street, New York, NY 10021-6595 (212) 734-2134.

Applicants must be full-time graduate or undergraduate (college level Juniors and Seniors) students who are either U. S. citizens of Polish descent, Poles with U. S. Permanent Resident status, or Americans pursuing the study of Polish subjects.

(343) Study/Travel Abroad. Rotary Foundation Scholarship, The Rotary Foundation of Rotary International, One

Rotary Center, 1560 Sherman Avenue, Evanston, Ill 60201, U.S.A. Grants awards are: maximum $2,500 or its equivalent for Academic-Year Scholarships.

The grant is $10,000 maximum or its equivalent per year for Multi-Year Scholarships for up to each of 3 years, $9,500 and $17,000 for three-month and six-month Cultural Scholarships, respectively.

(344) Study/Travel Abroad-Architecture. The American Institute of Architects/The American Architectural Foundation Scholarship Programs. The American Institute of Architects, 1735 New York Avenue, N. W., Washington, DC. 20006-5292. This is a program for foreign travel in conjunction with a professional degree is offered. Deadline: February 15 each year. Deadline: February 15 each year.

(345) Study/Travel Abroad-Graduate. Fulbright-Hays Seminars Abroad., CFDA #84.018 Contact: Linda Byrd-Johnson, Center for International Education, U. S. Department of Education (Room 3062) 7th & D Streets, S. W., Washington, DC 20202-5332 (202) 708-8294. To provide short-term (3-8 week) summer seminars abroad for qualified U. S. educators in the fields of the social sciences, the humanities, and social studies to improve their understanding and knowledge of the people and culture of another country(ies). Deadline: November 9, each year. Deadline: November 9, each year.

(346) Study/Travel Abroad-Social Science. Social Science Research Council, 605 Third Avenue, New York, NY, 10158 (212) 661-0280.

Provides numerous fellowships and grants for training and research at the graduate, dissertation and doctorate levels. Many awards sponsor field research in foreign countries.

(347) Study/Travel Abroad-Undergraduate. National Security Program, Institute of International Education/Washington, DC, 1400 K St. N. W., Washington, DC 20005, (202)

COLLEGE: HOW TO GET THERE AND GO FREE
962-8835.

(348) Teacher Education. Professionally Accredited Nontraditional Routes to Teaching. 2010 Massachusetts Avenue, N. W., Washington, DC 20036-1023. (202) 466-7496.

(349) Visual Arts-Undergraduate. National Endowment for the Arts, Visual Arts Program/Fellowships, Rm. 729, Nancy Hanks Center, 1100 Pennsylvania Ave., N. W., Washington, D. C. Write for application and guidelines.

(350) Women-Behavioral Studies. National Chamber of Commerce For Women, Scholarships and Research Grants for Women, Ten Waterside Plaza, Suite 6H, New York, NY 10010.

(351) Women-Biology Doctorate. National Science Foundation, 1800 G Street, N. W., Washington, DC 20550.

(352) Women-Biology Graduate. National Science Foundation, 1800 G Street, N. W., Washington, DC 20550.

(353) Women-Business Studies. Avon Products Foundation, Business & Professional Women's Foundation, 2012 Massachusetts Ave., N. W., Washington, DC 20036. Grants awards are $1,000 each. Deadline: April 15.

(354) Women-Business Studies. Sears Roebuck, Business & Professional Women's Foundation, 2012 Massachusetts Ave., N. W., Washington, DC 20036. Women must be enrolled in graduate business studies.

(355) Women-Chemistry Doctorate. National Science Bell Laboratories, Crawfords Corner Rd. Rm. 1E-213, Holmdel, NJ 07733-1988, (908) 949-4301. Deadline: January 15 each year. 6595 (212) 734-2134.

(356) Women-Chemistry Graduate. National Science Foundation, 1800 G Street, N. W., Washington, DC 20550.

(357) Women-Communications Graduate. National Federation Press Women, NFPW Scholarships, Box 99, Blue
(358) Women-Communications Science Graduate. A T & T Bell Laboratories, Crawfords Corner Rd. Rm. 1E-213, Holmdel, NJ 07733-1988, (908) 949-4301. Deadline: January

l5 each year. Grants awards are $1,000 for a professional member with a BA or BS and two years membership. Deadline: May l.

(359) Women-Communications Science Undergraduate.
A T & T Bell Laboratories, Crawfords Corner Rd. Rm. lE-2l3, Holmdel, NJ 07733-1988, (908) 949-430l. Deadline: January l5 each year.

(360) Women-Computer Science Doctorate, A T & T Bell Laboratories, Crawfords Corner Rd. Rm. lE-2l3, Holmdel, NJ 07733-1988, (908) 949-430l. Deadline: January l5 each year.

(361) Women-Computer Science Graduate. A T & T Bell Laboratories, Crawfords Corner Rd. Rm. lE-2l3, Holmdel, NJ 07733-1988, (908)949-430l. Deadline: January l5 each year.

(362) Women-Electronic Degrees. Electrical Women's Roundtable, P. O. Box 292793, Nashville, TN 37229-2793.

(363) Women-Electronic Degrees. Women in Electronics-Atlanta Chapter, P. O. Box 956213, Duluth, Georgia 30136. Scholarship awards are made to some women who will pursue careers in the high technology industry.

(364) Women-Engineering Doctorate. A T & T Bell Laboratories, Crawfords Corner Rd. Rm. lE-2l3, Holmdel, NJ 07733-1988, (908) 949-430l. Deadline: January l5 each year.

(365) Women-Engineering Graduate. Zonta International, Amelia Earhart Fellowship Awards, 557 West Randolph Street, Chicago, IL 60606. Criterion: You must have your bachelor's degree. (312) 930-5848, Fax: (312) 930-095l.

(366) Women-Engineering Graduate. A T & T Bell Laboratories, Crawfords Corner Rd. Rm. lE-2l3, Holmdel, NJ 07733-1988, (908) 949-430l. Deadline: January l5 each year.

(367) Women-Fellowships. Zonta International, Zonta Amelia Earhart Fellowship Awards, 557 West Randolph Street, Chicago, IL 60606. (312) 930-5848, Fax: (312) 930-095l.

(368) Women-General. Soroptimist Training Awards Program, Soroptimist International of the Americas, Inc., 1616 Walnut Street, Philadelphia, PA 19103. (215) 732-0512.

For women, preferably over 30 years old, who are either heads of households or have families dependent on them. Stipends for $3,500 are annually awarded to 54 recipients. Deadline: December 1, each year.

(369) Women-General. Clairol Scholarship Program. Business & Professional Women's Foundation, 2012 Massachusetts Avenue, N. W., Washington, DC 20036.

For women who are returning to education after having stopped higher education to give birth.

(370) Women-General Graduate. Miss America Pagent Scholarships, P. O. Box 119, Atlantic City, NJ 08404, (609) 345-7571. Criteria: (1) Applicant must be between the ages of 17-24 (2) single and never married (3) High school graduate. Combined annual scholarship awards exceed $10,000,000.

(371) Women-General Graduate. American Association of University Women Educational Foundation 1111-16th Street, N.W., Washington, DC 20006. (202)728-7603. Amounts vary. Deadline: August 1 each year. Additional grants are awarded to women teachers with 5-10 years of classroom experience teaching math or science to at-risk-girls. Request information about the Eleanor Roosevelt Fund For Women And Girls.

(372) Women-General Graduate. Patricia Roberts Harris Fellowships, ROB 3, Rm. 3022, 7th & D Streets, S. W., Washington, DC 20202-5251.

Criterion: You must be enrolled in a graduate degree program that is under-represented by women. The fund for these awards is $21, 780,000. Deadline: Varies

(373) Women-General Post-Doctorate. American Association of University Women Educational Foundation 1111-16th Street, N.W., Washington, DC 20006. (202)728-7603.

Amounts vary. Deadline: August 1 each year.

(374) Women-General Post-Graduate. American Association of University Women Educational Foundation 1111-16th Street, N. W., Washington, DC 20006. (202) 728-7603. Amounts vary. Deadline: August 1 each year.

(375) Women-General Undergraduate. Jeannette Rankin Foundation Awards, P. O. Box 6653, Athens GA 30604. From 7-10 one time awards for $1,000 are annually given to: (1) women 35 years or older (2) a U. S. citizen, and (3) accepted or enrolled in a certified program of technical/vocational training. Request application after September 1 and file before January 15.

(376) Women-Law African American. National Association of Negro Business and Professional Women's Clubs Scholarship Awards, 1806 New Hampshire Avenue, N. W. Washington, DC 20009.

(377) Women-Loans, Business Administration. Sears Roebuck, Business & Professional Women's Foundation, 2012 Massachusetts Ave., N. W., Washington, DC 20036. Criterion: Women must be enrolled in business graduate studies, loans are for $2,500 maximum.

(378) Women-Loans, Engineering Graduate Studies. Business & Professional Women's Foundation, 2012 Massachusetts Ave., N. W., Washington, DC 20036. Loans are available for women. Maximum is $5,000 each academic year.

(379) Women-Loans, Engineering Post-graduate Studies. Business & Professional Women's Foundation, 2012 Massachusetts Ave., N. W., Washington, DC 20036. Loans are available for women. Maximum is $5,000 each academic year.

(380) Women-Loans, Engineering Undergraduate Studies. Business & Professional Women's Foundation, 2012 Massachusetts Ave., N. W., Washington, DC 20036. Loans are available for women. Maximum is $5,000 each academic year.

(381) Women-Mathematics Doctorate. National Science Foundation, 1800 G Street, N. W., Washington, DC 20550.
(382) Women-Mathematics Graduate. National Science Foundation, 1800 G Street, N. W., Washington, DC 20550.
(383) Women-Mathematics Graduate. Sigma Delta Epsilon Fellowships, Graduate Women In Science, P. O. Box 19947, San Diego, CA 92120. (619) 583-4856. Stipends range from $1,500 to $4,000 each year for 4 recipients.
(384) Women-Medicine Undergraduate. AWHONN Education Fellowships, American Association of Women's Health, Obstetric and Neonatal Nurses, 700-14th St., N. W. Suite 600, Washington, DC 20005-2019. (202)863-2436. Deadline: April 16 each year.
(385) Women-Public Policy Research Graduate. The Women's Research And Education Institute, 1700 18th St., N. W., Washington, DC 20009, (202) 328-7070. Criteria: (1) You must be currently enrolled in a graduate studies program in order to apply for this award (2) complete a month-long orientation on women and public policy (3) Spend one academic year working in the offices of members of Congress or on congressional committee staffs, (4) spend 30 hours per week in your assigned offices.

You will receive 6 hours of arranged credit for the legislative and academic research you perform. Recipients are provided tuition and living stipend for the academic year (September through May). Deadline: March 15. Applications are available after November 1.
(386) Women-Public Policy Research Professional. The Women's Research And Education Institute, 1700 18th St., N. W., Washington, DC 20009, (202)328-7070. Criteria: (1) You must be currently enrolled in a graduate studies program in order to apply for this award, (2) you must be working in the area of public policy, (3) Spend one academic year working in the offices of members of Congress or on congressional committee staffs, (4) spend 30

hours per week in your assigned offices.

Recipients are provided tuition and living stipend for the academic year (September through May). Deadline: March 15. Applications are available after November 1.

(387) Women-Science Doctorate. National Science Foundation, 1800 G Street, N. W., Washington, D C 20550.

(388) Women-Science Graduate Zonta International, Zonta Amelia Earhart Fellowship Awards, 557 West Randolph Street, Chicago, IL 60606.

Criterion: You must have your bachelor's degree. (312)930-5848, Fax: (312)930-0951.

(389) Women-Science Graduate. National Science Foundation, 1800 G Street, N. W., Washington, DC 20550.

(390) Women-Science Graduate. Sigma Delta Epsilon Fellowships, Graduate Women In Science, P. O. Box 19947, San Diego, CA 92120. (619) 583-4856. Stipends range from $1,500 to $4,000 each year for 4 recipients.

(391) Women-Sorority. Beta Theta Pi Foundation, 208 East High Street, P. O. Box 6277, Oxford, OH 45056.

(392) Women-Sorority Graduate. Alpha Kappa Alpha Educational Advancement Foundation, 5656 S. Stony Island Avenue, Chicago, IL 60637, (312)947-0026 Fax: (312)947-0277. Grants awards are $500-1,500. Deadline: March 15.

(393) Women-Sorority Graduate. Zeta Phi Beta, 1734 New Hampshire Ave., Washington, DC 20009. For graduate women working on professional, masters, doctorate or enrolled in post-doctoral study.

Up to $2,500 per year. Request application and guidelines. Deadline: February 1.

(394) Women-Sorority Social Work. Mildred Carter Bradham Fellowship, Zeta Phi Beta Sorority, 1734 New Hampshire Ave., NW., Washington, DC 20009. $500-$1,000 for one academic year. Criterion: You must be a member. Deadline: February 1 each year.

(395) Women-Sorority Undergraduate. Alpha Kappa Al

pha Educational Advancement Foundation, 5656 S. StonyIsland Avenue, Chicago, IL 60637, (312)947-0026 Fax: (312)947-0277.

Applicants must have completed one full year of college education. Grants awards are $500-1,500. Deadline: March 15.

(396) Women-Technology Doctorate. National Science Foundation, 1800 G Street, N. W., Washington, DC 20550.

(397) Women - Technology Graduate. National Science Foundation, 1800 G Street, N. W., Washington, DC 20550.

(398) Women-Vocational / Technical. Jeannette Rankin Foundation Awards, P. O. Box 6653, Athens GA 30604..

From 7-10 one time awards for $1,000 are annually given to: (1) women 35 years or older (2) a U. S. citizen, and (3) accepted or enrolled in a certified program of technical/ vocational training. Request application after September 1 and file before January 15.

(399) Women-Whirly Girls. Doris Muellien Whirly Girls Scholarship, 7551 Callaghan Road, Suite 330, San Antonio, TX 78229. Must have had experience in piloting and helicopters.

(400) Women-Writers. National League of American Pen Women, Mature Women Scholarship Grants, 1300-17th Street, N. W., Washington, DC 20036. Awards are made to women who are aged 55 and over.

(401) Writing Assistance. The ADA Endowment and Assistance Fund, Inc., 211 East Chicago Avenue, Chicago, IL 60611-2678.

Criteria: (1) You must be a United States citizen (2) provide a written summary of your personal and professional goals and (3) send in 2-3 letters of reference. (4) You must have a minimum need of $2,500.

(402) Zoology-Graduate. National ZoologicalTraineeships, National Zoological Park, Washington, DC 20008 (202) 673-4950 Fax: (202) 673-4738.

••

Remember, *the purpose for this Chapter is to get you started on your grants search project. It is intended to get you accustomed to scrutinizing your sources for the best opportunities known to us to assist your getting higher education grants.*

••

You must pay attention to the general and specific grants, the contact persons, applications deadlines, amounts of awards and criteria.

If some of the grantors have either moved or changed their funding guidelines, reuse the book and let **Chapter Four, "Where To Find Information About Free College Money"** provide you guidance.

You will always have ideas for finding more sources. All financial aid money for education is estimated at more than $1,000,000,000 (ONE BILLION DOLLARS).

"Ms. Womack, Your book is still being used at our church. We often refer to it although it has been 6 years since we bought it."--D. S. Camden, NJ

"What one has to do usually can be done."
Anna Eleanor Roosevelt

CHAPTER EIGHT

College Survival Information.

Students, especially those who are first-generation college graduates often find themselves in need of guidance. One big mistake they make is to expect it from their college advisors. These college staff persons are advisors of courses to select and not necessarily to inform you of anything else.

You may need tips about how to get through higher education as easily as possible. They may be obtained from relatives, friends, coeds and campus bookstores.

College can successfully be approached if you perceive of it as a game. It is similar to sports or other activities where participants compete. Success requires your first becoming organized. Thereafter, you must learn the rules and regulations to master them.

Attendance.

After reading attendance regulations in more than seventy college catalogs, I found a unanimous expectation by colleges for students to regularly attend classes and on time. Although in reality, sometimes a professor may tell you attendance to class has no effect on your grades.

But,, if you want to question a grade, the professor will possibly say, "You should have attended class more!" Additionally, you may be told you missed a lot of information discussed in class during one of your absences.

When you do not attend, you lose the benefit of class participation. You miss additional information conveyed by your classmates and you miss the grade you may have anticipated getting.

Beware of theft.

Place your work under the professors' office doors. Do not leave your papers in your professors' mailboxes outside their office doors. They are sometimes stolen.

Your papers may show up as someone else's work. A thief in your class may report the same data you were turning in for grading.

Be humble.

Don't get puffed up and vain. It's okay to pat yourself on the back for work well done; but, do not become vain. If you discuss your ideas with people, they will give your ideas for test answers. The appearance to the professor will be you have cheated when you did not.

Where you may have gotten an "A" grade, you and the others with the same ideas and theories will each get a "B". Ideas, when given by many, are no longer original. You will get demerits.

Give up your thoughts only in class when you need points for class participation. Otherwise, sav e them for your written assignments. In other words, "If they are your ideas, you get the credit _for your ideas_!"

Bulletin boards.

Taking time to scan over bulletin boards on campus will produce additional sources of information for you. Some of the following can be found on them:

1. Employment opportunities
2. Used book sales
3. Schedules of lectures and conferences related to your course work-data to be quoted for term papers.
4. Current (and frequent) bureaucratic changes
5. Available scholarships/fellowships
6. Teaching assistantships offered within each graduate department.

The above listing reflects just a small amount of resources available to you.

Campus Advisors.

Your advisor may recommend courses to you. Question whether those courses are being chosen in a sequential order in their relationship to future required courses. If they are, it will be easier for you to relate and understand more of your course content.

College newspapers.

Read the college periodicals for resources. Also, you will keep abreast of campus events, opportunities and problems. Some of the information may be of importance to you.

Course catalogs.

If you are taking courses, read the descriptions printed in the catalogs. They may give you additional insight to what the course was intended to convey. The data can be used for a perspective/slant on either your thesis papers or essay questions.

Additionally, this is where class rules and regulations are listed. How can you excel if you do not know the process of how to succeed. How can you prevail well without knowing the little loop holes designed to be helpful you?

Course sequence.

It is suggested that you take your courses in sequence. This pertainstowhen courses are taken as well as the order they should be taken. Courses for which you are required to develop skills should be taken first if that skill must be used throughout your college career.

An example is your developing writing skills generally acceptable campus-wide. Enrolling in required English courses either upon admission or shortly thereafter (within the first year), helps you improve upon your writing abilities.

At some colleges, professors will grade your papers; but, they rarely correct your grammar. They tend to mainly focus on ideas. You will repeatedly make the same writing mistakes.

You will be doing yourself a favor by enrolling in your English courses within your freshman year.

Also, when you select some of the Liberal Arts courses, choose Biology, Anthropology and then Sociology. A pedagogical (step by step) order historically covers the evolution of mankind from the genetic structure, thru dinosaurs then to humans living in complex societies.

Think about the mental confusion you would cause yourself if you enrolled in the Sociology course before Biology!

You would be starting at the end of the human continuum as we know it. Thereby, some of the Sociological concepts may be unclear because you lack the knowledge about how human beings evolved and progressed to where we are today.

Get organized.

Get your assignments and other materials together. You must put aside definite study hours. A specific space with absolute quiet is needed for concentration.

If this cannot be obtained at home, go to either a campus or public library. "How To Study" courses recommend 2-3 hours weekly study for each course.

Course assignments are most often given to you at the first or second meeting for your course. Your using binders with pockets will increase your efficiency in meeting deadlines.

Binders will help you keep data for each course separated. Notes will be kept in their relative sections. Pockets will hold your syllabus and course related materials.

Read your syllabus before every class and before reviewing class notes. Then, all essays or reports will be given to your professors on or before their due dates. Otherwise, late assignments are likely to lower your grades.

Grading policies.

Currently, professors use assorted grading policies to arrive at grade levels for course work. The students gets a menu. Then he or she picks and chooses what will be used to either make up a 100-point score or what will be equal to an "A" grade.

Midterm Exam	10	points
Applied Project	30	points
In-class Presentation	20	points
Synthesis Activity	10	points
Draft and Final Paper	30	points
	100	points total

You may want to use the tasks to you the highest points. Others choose to use a number of smaller tasks requiring you to do many different projects. Try a combination, see what works best. The grading menu is extremely challenging.

Incompletes.

You should be aware of the regulations, requirements and time constraints relating to the Incomplete Grade referred to as an "I". Get this information from your college-catalog, registration office, and request the advice of other students.

College requirements are expectations for students to complete all of the obligations stipulated for a particular course. However, if at the end of the semester, a small portion of the work remains unfinished, it is deferred, an "I" or incomplete may be submitted.

Reasons such as serious illness, extenuating home circumstances, and unavailability of information, etc. are generally considered acceptable situations for professors to grant a student an "I". The due-date for the work is extended to some future time agreed upon by both the student and the professor.

You will find any student who completes an "I" grade on the first agreed upon date will be both a rare and unique person. Most often, students become anxious because they know their work will be graded one grade lower because it is late.

Thereafter, in an effort to be as near perfect as possible, the student continuously takes more and more time to add material to compensate for the lateness.

If you are a procrastinator, do not take the "I" grade at least not without knowing the date the "I's" automatically change to "F's" in your college's registration office.

Jargon.

A mastery of the terminology/jargon used in a course is a valuable asset. I had a discovery while successfully completing over 218 college credit hours. Studying the course jargon and learning it within the first two weeks of each semester, will give you an advantage in competing with other students.

First of all, you will be able to understand your professors' lectures when jargon will be used. Also, he "A" students use jargon when they ask and respond to questions.

Communicating using course jargon will likely convey you are interested in the course, you have been studying and you have developed knowledge of it. Knowledge of the course jargon will help you better understand examination questions; and, your grades will be higher.

By mid-semester when other students know the language related to the course, you will have already established the status of a "bright" student with the professor and your coeds (who are sometimes asked to grade you instead of the professor).

College is competitive, so learn the course jargon and you can become and remain in the forefront of the race toward top grades.

Libraries on Campus.

During the student-orientation program, you will usually be told about library resources and how to use them.

Two strategies will maximize your getting the library data when you want it.

Both are based upon your timing; specifically, when you begin to utilize the library and the hours. One reason you should use the campus library during the first two weeks of your first freshman semester is based upon your immediately overcoming any anxieties.

Many students avoid making their initial visit because they say they are overwhelmed by the massive amount of books, magazines, newspapers, etc. housed in the
libraries. They become intimidated by them.

It is suggested you will go to the library during the first week of <u>each</u> semester so you can have an excellent opportunity to get the books, articles, etc. before your classmates leave the shelves bare.

An added benefit is the money you save. Professors usually have copies of textbooks on loan in the reserve section. You can take advantage of reading the required text at no cost.

This is a money-saver tip especially valuable during this era of increasing textbook prices. You save money and time as well. You don't have to drive around to bookstores to purchase textbooks.

Why go to a library at a time when many of your classmates are attempting to answer the same course questions? You will be competing for the same books.

Use the libraries during hours unpopular and unattractive to other students. Many students will go to the libraries immediately after classes. Try attending later, such as late at night or early mornings for your best outcome.

When you want to minimize the competition for materials, visit the campus libraries on weekends and holidays too!

Remember, using the library during the first two weeks

of your first freshman semester will decrease anxiety about being overwhelmed.

Habitually going to the campus libraries during the first two weeks of each semester will increase the probability of your getting exactly what you are seeking. It will provide a savings to you.

Visit during the least opportune hours for others late nights, mornings and weekends.

Meeting People.

Beginning with the day of orientation thru graduation, you should make a habit of introducing yourself to at least one person in each campus group setting.

Most people are more than eager to share information. You increase and maximize your opportunities to be more informed when you meet other students, join organizations and clubs.

Also, you will greatly benefit from establishing communication with departmental secretaries. Having rapport with departmental secretaries helps you get in-depth information about your department.

You can also get an idea about which professors are more stern, demanding, fair, etc. Departmental secretaries can aid your contacting professors should an emergency arise. Show your appreciation with thank you cards, etc.

Meeting classmates, joining organizations, attending lectures and establishing a rapport with departmental secretaries will enable you to become a more informed student. Much of the information you receive can become resources for yourself and other students.

Professors.

An initial fear of professors in unwarranted. Your professors can especially be approached when you want an overenrolled or closed class, need a due-date extension or to debate your grades.

When you find a course is closed because of over-enrollment. Approach the professor of the class you want. Simply tell the professor you need his or her class because the hours permit you to work, or the course is not offered the next semester.

Whatever the reason, be honest! The professor usually will permit you to enter the class by signing the necessary registration forms.

Often, professors will permit you to take a one-day extension to submit a class assignment. To avoid being penalized and receive a lowered grade, you should find out what the professor considers "late work."

Sometimes, only several hours extension will give you time to submit your best work and be free of either typing errors or other mistakes.

Professors are willing to hear sound debates for higher grades. Excellent attendance and maximum/quality class participation are variables to use. A professor may increase a C+ to a B-grade.

Professors will help you with any classroom or course-related problems. Approach a professor to get a class you need during a particular semester, to get an assignment due date extended or to debate your grade.

Most often, professors are generally more kind, considerate and approachable than students usually think. Never be shy about asking any professor for any request of benefit to you. More often than not, the answer is yes, and your request is granted. Be brave and ask.

Developing courage is an asset. Courage also helps you get a job, a better job and a pay increase. You must have courage to ask.

Study

No matter how great the demands or how hard the work, you must study. Always remember, the main contribution you can give to yourself, your career, and to your life is to study at least 2 hours nightly. This must be done from the time you enter high school.

Begin each semester and each course with the same amount of commitment. If your homework can be completed in one hour, read several chapters ahead in your textbooks. Your reading levels, vocabulary and knowledge of the subjects will increase.

You will rapidly develop a grasp of the entire course. You will be more creative in your essays. What was at one time a "C " - "B" average will become B to A-grades. Love yourself, sacrifice early and later reap many, many unexpected rewards.

Study Groups.

Students will form support systems in an effort to get through a difficult course. One of those is called a study group. It is comprised of students who review complex concepts and share in answering questions related to exams.

Often, about five students will meet to share their individual knowledge and ideas about a course for the betterment of the group.

Unclear theories and complex concepts are thought out and discussed among the members of the group until the work is understood.

Members of other study groups will divide essay questions among members. When the group meets at a later time, each student will get the answers to remaining questions, e.g.,

If there are 10 questions in the essay exam, each of the five students will take two questions to answer. At the designated meeting time and place, each member will have five copies of his or her questions and answers.

Those are traded until each student has a copy of all ten questions and answers to the exam. Beware! One problem can be created by using this method of study.

Answering questions within a collective study group

may be a disadvantage because other students may not be as thorough as you.

THINK ABOUT IT, people do not usually record information they already know; for example, a person who knows what historically happened between World War I and the stock market crash on October 29, 1929, may exclude that data from an answer.

The result is, your answer to that question in the exam is incomplete. Rather, you should participate with the study group *to enhance your own independent study* for the exam. Thereafter, a high grade should be your reward.

It is another way to reinforce the data you glean from repetition. Test the methods of study group involvement to discern whether there i s a benefit to you.

Withdrawals.

Sometimes you will find you are not going to do well in a course. Learn your college or university's rules regarding withdrawals from courses.

You will be able to use them as resources to save yourself from failure and to retrieve money paid for unwanted courses.

You may find you are failing a course, a withdrawal is used to avoid an "F" grade. Never withdraw from a course without submitting the required forms to your registration or bursar's office.

If you withdraw from a course within a specified amount of time after the semester begins, the college or university will usually refund a percentage of the course costs.

Maybe it will be better for your circumstances withdrawing rather than your receiving a failing grade and lowering your grade-point average. The university will usually refund a percentage of the course.

If you can afford to forfeit the money, you may consider reenrolling in the course rather than receiving the"F"-

grade. You must judge what is the most beneficial to your finances, time and other constraints.

Conclusion.

Your college career can be most successful if you start by acquainting yourself with the rules and regulations on your campus.

You can increase your chances of survival if you take heed to the following: campus advisors, class attendance, beware of theft; reading bulletin boards; reading college newspapers; keeping course catalogs; choosing sequential courses; getting organized; assessing grading policies; gaining knowledge of incompletes; learning the course jargon; using the libraries on campus; meeting people, professors, study, assessing study groups and getting the current information about withdrawals.

This information is made available to you for your advantage. Use it and great success should be yours.

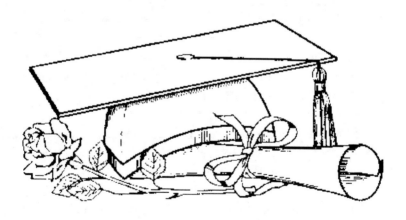

"The Lord will perfect that which concerneth me; thy mercy. O' Lord, endureth forever; forsake not the works of thine own hands." Psalm 138: Verse 8.

BIBLIOGRAPHY OF
FINANCIAL AID DIRECTORIES

The Electronic University: *A Guide To Distance Learning Programs.* Peterson's Guides, P. O. Box 2123, Princeton, NJ 08543-2123. Cost: $15.95.

AFL-CIO Guide To Union Sponsored *Scholarships, Awards, and Student Financial Aid.* AFL-CIO Department of Education, 815 - 16th St., N. W. Room 407, Washington, DC 20006. 1996 ed. Cost: Free to union members and $3 to others.

Annual Register of Grant Support. This book contains the names of nearly 2,900 organizations and institutions with student aid money. Academic Media, Los Angeles, CA.

Assistantships And Graduate Fellowships In The Mathematical Sciences. American Mathematical Society (AMS) P. O. Box 6248, Providence, RI 02940. Free: postage and handling $4.

Chronicle Student Aid Annual. It contains information on financial aid programs offered nationally or regionally, primarily by noncollegiate organizations, public and private. Provides descriptions of more than 1,500 loans, grants, scholarships, fellowships, competitions, contests, and internships, 280 pp. Chronicle Guidance Publications, Inc. P. O. Box 1190, Moravia, New York 13118-1190, or call (315)497-0330. Cost: $22.

Bear, John. *College Degrees By Mail (1995).* Ten Speed Press, P.O. Box 7123, Berkeley, CA 94707 211 pp. Cost: $12.95.

Complete College Financing Guide. Prepared by Marguerite J. Dennis. Main emphases is federal and state funding, 251 pp. (Available from: Barron's Educational Series, 250 Wireless Blvd., Hauppauge, NY 11788). Cost: $13.95

Complete College Financing Guide 2nd. Edition. Barron's Educational Series, Inc., 250 Wireless Boulevard,

COLLEGE: HOW TO GET THERE AND GO FREE
Hauppauge, NY 11788. ISBN 0-8120-4950-0.

Corporation for Public Broadcasting works with colleges and universities to provide courses over public broadcasting stations: Write the Annenberg CPB Project, 901 E St., N. W., Washington, DC 20004, Phone: (202) 879 9657

Directory of Financial Aid for Minorities., 668 pp. Reference Service Press. San Carlos, CA. 1996-97. Cost: $47.50.

Directory of Financial Aid for Women., 504 pp. Reference Service Press. San Carlos, CA. 1996-97. Cost: $45.00.

Directory of Media Programs. Included is information on degrees offered, program size, application deadline, tuition costs, graduate assistantships, facilities, curriculum, faculty, etc. Broadcast Education Association 1771 N. Street, NW, Washington, DC 20036. Cost: $15.

Directory of Special Programs for Minority Group Members: Career Information Services, Employment Skills Banks & Financial Aid Sources. A 350-page book on college scholarship sources and information. Garrett Press, P. O. Box 190-A, Garrett Park, MD 20896.

Don't Miss Out: The Ambitious Student's Guide To Financial Aid. Prepared by Robert Leider and Anna Leider. (Available from: Octameron Press, P. O. Box 2748, Alexandria, VA 22301.) 117 pp. Cost for the 1994-95 edition: $7 Strategies for seeking financial aid on the undergraduate level, federal and state grants sources providing "Federal Benefits For Veterans And Dependents."

This booklet provides a summary of benefits available to veterans and their dependents from the federal government.

Updated annually, it contains information on aid for the blind, compensation for service connected disabilities, dental treatment, veterans' education and training loans, medical benefits & etc. Available from: Superintendent of Documents, U. S. Government Printing Office, Washington, DC 20402. Cost: $2.75.

Financial Aid For The Disabled And Their Families. 322 pp. (Available from: Reference Service Press, 1100 Industrial Rd., Suite 0, San Carlos, CA 94070). 1994-96 ed. Cost: $38.50. Nearly 800 funding opportunities established to assist persons with disabilities, their children or parents with scholarships, fellowships, loans, grants-in-aid, awards and internships.

Financial Aid For Minorities In Journalism/Mass Communications. Garrett Park Press, P. O. Box 190B, Garrett Park, MD 20896: (301)946-2553. Cost: $4.00

Foundation Grants to Individuals., Foundation Center 79 5th Avenue, New York, NY 10003-3076. 1(800)424-9836.

Funding For U. S. Study: A Guide For Foreign Nationals. This book advises students on planning for financial aid and describes over 600 grants and fellowships open to foreign nationals in varying fields of studies and countries of origin. Cost: $39.95 plus $4.00 shipping ($16 shipping overseas). Institute of International Education, 809 United Nations Plaza, New York, NY 10017-3580.

Gale's Encyclopedia of Associations. Provides details on nearly 21,000 national and international non-profit trade and professional associations. Scholarships lists 1,350 national, local and regional funds. For information about either book, contact: Gale Research, Inc. 835 Penobscot Bldg., Detroit MI 48226-4094.

Graduate Scholarship Book. This directory lists 1,600 scholarships, fellowships, grants and other financial aid opportunities. National Scholarship Research Service, Prentice Hall, Inc., NJ 1995. "Guide To Federal Funding For Education" Government Information Services 1611 N. Kent Street, Suite 508, Arlington, VA 22209. Cost: $248.

Guide To Federal Funding For Government And Non -Profits. Government Information Services 1611 N. Kent Street, Suite 508, Arlington, VA 22209. Cost: $249.

Journalist's Road to Success: A Career and Scholarship

Guide. This book has a listing of all known journalism scholarships (more than $3 million). Over 3,000 journalism students each year make use of these scholarships. Make checks payable to Dow Jones Newspaper Fund, P. O. Box 300, Princeton, NJ 08543-0300 or call 1(800) Dow-Fund. Cost: $3

Mecklermedia's Official Internet World Wide Web Yellow Pages., IDG Books Worldwide, Inc. 919 East Hillsdale Boulevard Suite 400, Foster City, CA 94409.

Need A Lift? 126 pp. Available from: American Legion, P. O. Box 1055, Indianapolis, IN 46206.) 1994 ed. This is intended primarily as a source book for children of veterans and some are also for veterans' spouses. Cost: $2.00

Scholarships And Grants For Study Or Research In U. S. A., A Scholarship Handbook For Foreign Nationals. Information on financing studies in the United States with sections on receiving financial aid from U.S. colleges, foundations and international organizations. American Collegiate Service, P. O. Box 442008, Houston, TX 77244. Cost: $23.95 plus $1.40 U.S. shipping or $5.50 overseas.

Selected List of Fellowship Opportunities & Aids to Advanced Education. Guide to sources for graduates at the Master, Doctorate and Post-doctorate levels. The Publications Office, National Science Foundation Center, 1800 G Street, NW, Washington, D. C. 20550. (202)357-9859, or (703)306-1234. Publication No. NSF 88-119.

Sources Of Financial Aid Available to American Indian Students. Fifty pages listing scholarships from government and private sources. Indian Resources Development (IRD) New Mexico State University, P. O. Box 30001, Dept. IRD, Las Cruces, NM 88003. 1(505)646-1347. Superintendent of Documents, U. S. Government Printing Office, Washington, DC 20404. For private foundation funding. Arrowstar Publishing, 10134, University Park Station, Denver, CO 80210-0134. ISBN# 0-935151-24-9.

BIBLIOGRAPHY OF FINANCIAL
AID DIRECTORIES

The American Indian/Alaska Native Higher Education Funding Guide. Includes information on grants, government funding and private foundation funding. Arrowstar Publishing, 10134, University Park Station, Denver, CO 80210-0134. ISBN#0-935151-24-9.

The College Handbook - Foreign Student Supplement. Includes facts for undergraduate and graduate foreign students on enrollment, TOEFL, application deadlines, foreign students services, and housing at many U. S. institutions plus financial aid data. College Board Publications, Box 886, New York, NY 10101-0886 for $16.00 plus $8.31 for overseas shipping.

The Grants Register. Primarily intended for students at or above the graduate level who require further professional or advanced vocational training. St. Martin's Press, 175 Fifth Avenue, New York, NY 10010. The Scholarship Book: Complete Guide To Private Sector Scholarships, Grants & Loans For Undergraduates. A 400 page listing of various financial aid resources. National Scholarship Research Service 2280 Airport Blvd., Santa Rosa, CA 95403.

The Students Guide To Five Federal Financial Aid Programs. Federal Financial Aid, P. O. Box 84, Washington, DC 20044. FREE.

"Education's purpose is to replace an empty mind with an open one." - Malcolm S. Forbes

"Do not postpone your life."
Ralph Waldo Emerson

INDEX OF GRANTS SOURCES

COLLEGE: HOW TO GET THERE AND GO FREE
AMERICAN JEWISH JOINT DISTRIBUTION
    COMMITTEE
AMERICAN OCCUPATIONAL THERAPY
    FOUNDATION
AMERICAN POLITICAL SCIENCE ASSOCIATION
AMERICAN SOCIETY OF NEWSPAPER EDITORS
    FOUNDATION
AMERICAN SOCIOLOGICAL ASSOCIATION
AMERICAN VETERANS (AMVETS)
APPLEBAUM SCHOLARSHIPS
ARTS SCHOLARSHIPS
ASIAN AMERICAN JOURNALISTS ASSOCIATION
AT & T
AVIS RENT-A-CAR SCHOLARSHIPS
AVON PRODUCTS FOUNDATION
BETA THETA PI
BROADCAST PIONEERS SCHOLARSHIP
BUREAU OF HEALTH PUBLIC RESEARCH/HEALTH
    RESEARCH STUDENTS' ASSISTANCE
BUSINESS & PROFESSIONAL WOMEN'S
    FOUNDATION
CHRISTIAN WOMEN'S SCHOLARSHIPS
CLAIROL SCHOLARSHIP PROGRAM
COCOA-COLA FOUNDATION
COLLEGE ENTRANCE EXAMINATION BOARD
COLLEGE LEVEL EDUCATIONAL
    OPPORTUNITY(CLEO)
COLLEGE SCHOLARSHIP INFORMATION BANK
COMMITTEE ON SCHOLARLY COMMUNICATIONS
    WITH CHINA
COOPERATIVE DEVELOPMENTAL ENERGY
    PROGRAM
COUNCIL FOR INTERNATIONAL EXCHANGE OF
    SCHOLARS
COUNCIL ON INTERNATIONAL EDUCATION

KRAFT GENERAL FOODS FOUNDATION
HERBERT LEHMAN SCHOLARSHIPS
LIPTON FOUNDATION
LULAC NATIONAL EDUCATION SERVICE CENTER
MANEELY FUND, INC.
ROLAN D. MELTON FELLOWSHIPS
MEMORIAL FOUNDATION FOR JEWISH CULTURE
MISS AMERICA PAGENT SCHOLARSHIPS
DOROTHY MUELLIEN WHIRLY-GIRLS
    SCHOLARSHIP
NABISCO FOODS
NATIONAL ASSOCIATION OF BLACK JOURNALISTS
NATIONAL ASSOCIATION OF BROADCAST
    EDUCATION
NATIONAL ASSOCIATION OF BROADCASTERS
NATIONAL ASSOCIATION OF HISPANIC
    JOURNALISTS
NATIONAL ASSOCIATION OF NEGRO BUSINESS
    AND PROFESSIONAL WOMEN'S CLUBS
    SCHOLARSHIP AWARDS
NATIONAL ASSOCIATION OF RETURNING
    STUDENTS
NATIONAL CHAMBER OF COMMERCE FOR WOMEN
NATIONAL ENDOWMENT FOR THE ARTS
NATIONAL FEDERATION OF PRESS WOMEN
NATIONAL FRATERNAL SOCIETY OF DEAF
    SCHOLARSHIP
NATIONAL HEALTH SERVICE CORPS
NATIONAL HISPANIC SCHOLARSHIP FUND
NATIONAL INSTITUTES OF HEALTH
NATIONAL MEDICAL FELLOWSHIPS, INC.
NATIONAL LEAGUE OF AMERICAN PEN WOMEN
NATIONAL NEWSPAPER FOUNDATION
NATIONAL NEWSPAPER PUBLISHERS ASSOCIATION
    GRANTS

COLLEGE: HOW TO GET THERE AND GO FREE
SOCIAL SCIENCE RESEARCH COUNCIL
SOCIETY OF ACTUARIES
SOCIETY OF ENVIRONMENTAL GEOLOGISTS
SOROPTOMIST INTERNATIONAL OF THE
     AMERICAS, INC.
EDITH M. STRONG FOUNDATION
HARRY S. TRUMAN SCHOLARSHIP FOUNDATION
UNITED METHODISTS COMMUNICATION GRANTS
UNITED STATES DEPARTMENT OF EDUCATION
UNITED STATES DEPARTMENT OF ENERGY
UNITED STATES DEPARTMENT OF HEALTH &
     HUMAN SERVICES
UNITED STATES DEPARTMENT OF THE ARMY
UNITED STATES DEPARTMENT OF THE NAVY UNI-
VERSITY COPORATION FOR ATMOSPHERIC
     RESEARCH
WESLEYAN UNIVERSITY
WESTERN GOLF ASSOCIATION
WESTINGHOUSE SCIENCE TALENT SEARCH
WOMEN IN ELECTRONICS
WOMEN'S RESEARCH AND EDUCATION INSTITUTE
WOODROW WILSON NATIONAL FELLOWSHIP
     FOUNDATION
ZETA PHI BETA SORORITY
ZONTA INTERNATIONAL AMELIA EARHART
     FELLOWSHIP AWARDS

"Well done is better than well said."
-Benjamin Franklin

LOVE YOUR - SELF...

Have confidence that if you have done a little thing well, you can do a bigger thing well, too."---Storey

"It's easy to stand with the crowd; it takes courage to stand alone."
Anonymous

INDEX OF GRANTS
SUBJECTS/CATEGORIES

COLLEGE: HOW TO GET THERE AND GO FREE

INDEX OF GRANTS SUBJECTS/ CATEGORIES

COLLEGE: HOW TO GET THERE AND GO FREE

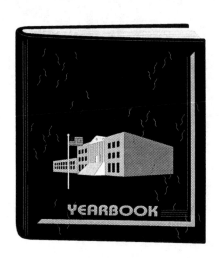

"We should all be concerned about the future because we will have to spend the rest of our lives there."
Charles Kettering

You need this book of hidden tips and strategies for entering college--it literally has been applauded by thousands! Included are: **Steps to College; how to write your entrance essays; review, respond to application questions; and locate free college money at more than 35 known places including some e-sites, How To Find and Apply For Grants, Scholarships, Fellowships, Over 400 Grants Sources, Includes Women, Minorities, Travel, Grants Criteria, Search Questions, Demographic Match Tips, Survival Information Strategies,** etc.

Plus... more than 400 sources to begin your search. Learn valuable skills such as: **How to survive college, increase your opportunities to get A & B grades. and much, much, more. <u>Get your copy *NOW*!</u>** Let this book guide you and your career into the Twenty-first Century.!

Additional Titles

WELFARE ENDED: AUGUST 22, 1996
by: Idalah D, Womack, School Social Worker

Implications for participants of the Federal Personal Responsibility and Work Opportunity Reconciliation Act of 1996 or Temporary Assistance to Needy Families. Impact to changes in cities, community based organizations, employment prospects, families as we knew them and individuals. Cost is $15.00 plus $3.00 shipping and handling.

POETRY FOR BEYOND THE YEAR 2,000: We Didn't Come To Stay   by: George Handsome

Depictions of environments from rolling hills to the drunk house.   Direct, striking and straight to the heart. Cost is $15.00 plus $3.00 shipping and handling.

Title(s)_____

_____

Name_____

Address_____

City_____State_____Zip_____

Telephone NO_____

Send to: ENLIGHTENMENT PUBLICATIONS
900 N, 19th St. #3237
PHILADELPHIA, PENNSYLVANIA
toll free number: 1-888-535-6160
fax: 1-609-871-6160
e-mail: acollegehowto@home.com